WEST VIEW PARK

WEST VIEW PARK

The Story of the
T.M. HARTON COMPANY

Mike Funyak

Color Edition – 2nd Printing
ISBN: 979-8-218-52042-7
Library of Congress Control Number: 2024920545

Cover Design by Jason Price
Layout and Design by Jason Price

Front cover photos:
Color 1970s photo of Dips courtesy of Frank Czuri
Color Postcard of Danceland Entrance with Guests courtesy of Carol McIlvain

Contents

Preface

This book initially started as a research project to learn more about "The Other Park in Pittsburgh" and to one day write a book on the subject. Western Pennsylvania has a rich history in the amusement park industry, and for seventy-one years, Pittsburgh, Pennsylvania, was the home of two of the best operated parks in the country.

Some of the industry's earliest pioneers and innovators were either from, or jump-started their careers in, Pittsburgh. The story of West View Park and the T.M. Harton Company is just that. The Harton Family and T.M. Harton Company played an important role in shaping the amusement industry so many people love today. The amusement park industry is a business of love and can be quite emotional at times, especially for those who owned and managed their own park. A great deal of time and dedication is spent to assure that others can participate safely and enjoyably.

This book is meant to be an in-depth look into the amusement industry and how one family helped build the foundation of one of the world's most successful parks. Western Pennsylvania is home to many success stories in the amusement park industry. The Hartons were not alone. The McSwigan, Henninger, Comstock, and Pearce families are four more examples of success stories that cannot go without mention. To this day, individuals working in the amusement industry across the country call Pittsburgh, Pennsylvania, home. These families helped pave the way for many individuals who decided to follow a career in the amusement industry.

Acknowledgements

This book would not be possible without generous support from the Harton/Beares families, who greatly helped make this book a reality. While a lot of the information from the early years of the T.M. Harton Company and West View Park are lost to time, Janet Harton Von Twistern, Dr. George Harton IV, and Charles Beares III supplied a lot of detailed information that was used in this book. The amount of information and material shared about their family for this book was endless. I also want to thank Carol McIlvain, whose parents, Margaret and Harry Habel, worked at West View Park, for sharing her insight and memories with me. I am grateful for the time spent in compiling and sharing information, stories, memories, and photos used throughout this book. Without the support and insight from these individuals, this project would not have been possible. Unfortunately, not every story and photo were included in the book, but every effort was made to rediscover and capture the magic behind West View Park and the T.M. Harton Company.

Thank you to the former West View Park employees with whom I had the pleasure of speaking: Kathy Vettel Hilton, Jack Nofsinger, Tom "Benny" Benson, Scott "Scooter" Kerr, Larry Park, Jim Miller, Jean Burns MacDonald, L.

Howard Adams, Ron Beck, Rich Wahlster, Mary Ann Walter, Al Seitz, Elaine Bahr Macdonald, Ron Westerman, J.R. Henry, Tom Binz, and Albert Snyder.

Kathy Vettel Hilton was a key source in providing family photos and great stories about how her family (Great Uncle Erwin Vettel, Grandfather Ed A. Vettel Sr., Uncle Ed E. Vettel, and Father Bob "Bud" Vettel) was instrumental in the success of the T.M. Harton Company, West View Park, and Kennywood. Kathy, a member of her family's third of four generations to work in the amusement industry, was excited to talk about her family's contributions to the amusement park industry and advancement of the modern-day roller coaster. While the book focuses on the Harton family, it also tells the story of how the Vettel family became involved in the amusement industry and trusted leaders. In addition, I want to thank Erwin Vettel, son of Andrew Vettel Sr. and grandson of Erwin Vettel, for providing information about his family, grandfather, and father.

Jack Nofsinger fondly remembered West View Park and his time maintaining the West View Park carousel as well as providing artwork throughout the facility. With the help of former West View Park employee Tom Binz, this book showcases a number of photos from Nofsinger's personal collection.

Tom "Benny" Benson and Albert Snyder provided a large series of photographs for the book as well as a great deal of information and details only a former employee would know. The stories and memories provided by the former West View Park employees interviewed for this book helped tell the later chapters of the story.

I would also like to thank the following individuals for their assistance in making this book possible.

Paul McTighe, who provided information about his family's involvement at Kennywood and with the independent football league team that played home games at West View Park from 1919–1932.

Paul and Bridget Zern, who allowed me to view their collection of Western Pennsylvania amusement park memorabilia and information. This book features a number of items collected by the couple over the years pertaining to West View Park.

Mike Costello, who provided photos for the book and a great deal of information about the Western Pennsylvania Amusement Park scene. Mike also helped with selecting the photos used in the book.

Sam Shurgott provided detailed knowledge of the industry, ride manufacturers, and individuals who were associated with parks in the Western Pennsylvania region. He also assisted in helping outline the proper narrative of the story and provided information as to how the amusement industry evolved from its humble beginnings. Sam contributed his in-depth knowledge about Ed Vettel's design work, which he learned from Don Schanz, who worked in the maintenance department at Idora Park and Conneaut Lake Park, maintaining Ed Vettel's Idora Park Jack Rabbit, Baby Wildcat, and Conneaut Lake's Blue Streak.

Andy Quinn, whose family owned and operated Kennywood for more than a hundred years, provided industry insight and information about the relationship that existed between West View Park, Conneaut Lake Park, and Kennywood, along with numerous stories of the Pittsburgh amusement scene in the early 1900s and up through the closing of West View Park. He also assisted in answering many questions in a manner that showcased honesty about the nature of the amusement industry from an operator and owner point of view. A mentor in many ways, his support and guidance not only helped to shape the story of this book, but it helped my professional career as well.

In addition, thank you to the following individuals who contributed to this book:

Theresa Balzer, Beth Schellhaas, John Schalcosky, Brian Butko, Josh Litvik, B. Derek Shaw, Frank Czuri, Bill Henninger, Dick Knoebel, Fred Musso, Steve Valenti, Scott Crider, Carl Crider Jr., and the numerous individuals who have talked to me about this project and/or shared their personal memories of West View Park with me.

Another special thank you is extended to the Eberly Family Special Collections Library staff at Penn State University, to Gil Pietrzak and staff at the Carnegie Library of Pittsburgh, Pennsylvania Department, and the Pittsburgh Photographic Library for their assistance and support given during the research process.

Thank you to the wonderful staff at Word Association Publishers; Dr. Tom Costello, his wife Francine, my editor Pam Greer, and designer Jason Price. Their support and interest in the T.M. Harton Company story helped greatly in making this book reality. I never imagined I'd one day become a published author and with their help, made it reality.

Finally, this book would not be possible without the continued love and support from my parents and family. Thank you for always encouraging me every day to be the best person I can be. I'd like to thank my parents and my maternal grandparents, Vito and Mary Alioto, for introducing me to West View Park.

This book is for the Harton, Beares, and Vettel families and for all who have special memories of West View Park. To all the families who did or currently own, operate their own amusement parks or related businesses, thank you for your commitment to the magic of family entertainment.

Foreword

by: Janet Harton Von Twistern

with input from Charles Beares III

When I received an email from Mike, out of the blue, that he was interested in writing about the T.M. Harton Company and West View Park and the family that created them, I was so surprised, dumbfounded, really. Here was a young guy with a great love for amusement parks that stemmed from his grandparents, who met at West View Park, and his pursuit of working in the industry. I was immediately willing to help him but wasn't exactly sure how much help I could be, as my family never shared much about my grandfather, George Harton II, and his siblings. But I knew that I wanted to be involved and see where this went.

One of my earliest memories of West View Park is of my father, George M. Harton III, dragging me on the iconic Dips, even though I did not meet the height requirement, but the employees would not say no to him. So, up we'd go, slowly ascending that first gigantic hill that approached the white gazebo-like structure at the pinnacle. I knew that all hell would break loose once the train released itself from the chain and careened down, down, down, at a breath-taking speed before it sailed up to the top of the next hill. As I was thrown around the big curve and the other smaller hills, I realized I loved it!

As a young boy, my father had a similar first experience on the Dips, not only strapped in, but held onto tightly by his beloved Aunt Dada (Olive Harton Jones), his father's older sister.

When I was very young, I hardly understood the family involvement, but as I hit junior high, I began to realize how much people loved the park. On the days when tickets were being sold at school for our school picnic, I would have to hide or not go to school, as everyone wanted free tickets. By this time, I loved going as often as possible with friends.

The T.M. Harton Company, from 1893 to 1980, and West View Park Company were always a family owned and operated business. All three of us in the third generation—my brother George M. Harton IV, our cousin Charles L. Beares III, and I—grew up working in this exciting, unique environment. We loved every moment of it and learned a lot in the process.

I worked in the office seven days a week, from 4 p.m. till closing, answering phones, working on payroll, filling out reports, and helping anyone in the office. My brother George was stuck the first year in a windowless room counting tickets taken for each ride. He then went on to announce in the radio tower and live shows and eventually worked with the assistant manager.

Rock and roll came in the fifties and sixties, and to look out my window and see the midway full of people stopping everything they were doing and do the Twist was so amazing. Nothing like that had ever happened before. I was the perfect age for this, and I loved seeing and meeting everyone that I could.

I also loved the free acts and became very good friends with some of the entertainers, mainly Professor Keller and his wild animals and the Outten family of divers. I was slowly but surely getting bitten with the bug of wanting to continue in the family business. I started talking to my father about this more, and he was so happy to know how much I loved it. It was his last wish that the park continue, for it really was the love of his life.

The management of the companies can be broken down roughly into three periods of about equal duration. The early years occurred from 1893–1920, when my great uncle T.M. Harton (Uncle Marsh) founded and ran both the T.M. Harton Company and West View Park Company. In early 1919, Uncle Marsh succumbed to the worldwide Spanish Flu epidemic. Marsh's brother, George M. Harton II, my grandfather, assumed management, largely assisted by his half-sister Jessie's husband, Charles L. Beares, who handled the day-today responsibilities. Charles Beares, Sr. had been Uncle Marsh's right-hand man running our amusement business. Sadly, my grandfather died after a fierce struggle with an incurable cancer in 1920, not long after the death of his older brother.

The years 1920–1946 were considered the Beares era, aptly recounted here by Mike Funyak. My great aunts, Olive Harton Jones and Jessie Saint Beares, along with her husband, Charles, Sr., scraped up the wherewithal to buy out Laura Harton, Uncle Marsh's difficult widow. The three of them together ran the parent company and its subsidiaries until Olive's death in late December 1945. Jessie's and Charles' son, Charles L. Beares II, began managing West View Park shortly after his graduation from Princeton University in 1926. Over the years, Charles II gained a reputation among his peers as one of the savviest amusement park managers in the industry.

During the first half of the 1930s, my father's first cousin, Charles L. Beares II, and western film idol Tom Mix both married sisters from the renowned circus family the Flying Wards. Charles married Inez Hubbell Ward, at that time the only female catcher in a flying act. Tom Mix married Mable Hubbell Ward, famous for her daring flights on the flying trapeze and also for her center ring performances of one-arm swings.

Shortly before her death, Olive had created two rather complicated trusts holding her T.M. Harton stock with my brother George IV, Charles Beares III, and I as the beneficiaries. Although Charles Sr. and Jessie together had more T.M. Harton stock than Olive, Olive was the largest single stockholder.

My grandmother, Carice Harton Kountz, now married for the fourth time, would always vote her minority position against her former sister-in-law and brother-in-law, of whose management she never approved. She inherited her T.M. Harton stock from my grandfather. Carice used her votes and the trusts to unseat the Beareses from power, at least until the next annual stockholders' meeting. Jessie and Charles Beares Sr. were woefully unprepared at the March 1946 stockholders' meeting for the surprising coup d'etat they never saw coming. They never dreamed they would be voted out of power. Discouraged and bitter, Jessie and Charles Beares eventually sold out to Carice Kountz, which placed my grandmother in firm majority control and rendered Olive's two trusts meaningless.

From 1946 until 1966, when my father, George M. Harton III died, he and his mother ran the T.M. Harton Company and its subsidiaries. From 1966 until the dissolution of the companies, my grandmother and her fourth husband, prominent Pittsburgh Attorney A. Edward Kountz, managed the organization, aided by Jack Hickey, their longtime on-the-ground manager, and Margaret Habel, who worked in the office.

As I read what Mike has written, I am fascinated with the history lesson of my family. I really had no idea of all that they did. Why it was such a secret, I don't know, but maybe part of it was that families weren't into histories the way we are today with Ancestry, 23 and Me, and more.

I am so grateful to Mike for his endeavor and can't thank him enough. My hope (and desire) is that many people enjoy his tribute.

Chapter 1

Origins of the T.M. Harton Company

The scene in 1800s Pittsburgh, Pennsylvania was ever changing. The city and region were well known for their wealth of natural resources. Soon, foundries and mills appeared along the city's three major rivers: the Monongahela, the Allegheny, and the Ohio. Before the railroads opened in 1854, the city's three rivers were the major means of early transportation. By the late 1800s, the industrial revolution came to Pittsburgh in the form of manufacturing, and the city attracted families immigrating from all over the world. Prior to this period, the George Maurice Harton family came to the city from Ireland, having previously emigrated from England.

Harton founded the G.M. Harton & Company, one of the earliest transportation companies in Pittsburgh in the days of the Erie Canal. The company provided

Theodore Marshall (T.M.) Harton II

1

transportation between Pittsburgh and the eastern cities. Using steamboats on rivers and lakes, the company prided itself on providing passengers the most affordable and enjoyable route and experience.

Son Theodore Marshall (T.M.) Harton became interested in his father's business and later became a captain for the fleet. In January 1866, Theodore Marshall Harton established T.M. Harton & Company. The successor company of Long & Duff, T.M. Harton & Company manufactured various ropes, yarns, and twines. Following Harton's passing in October 1866, his surviving business partners formed a new co-partnership company, Evans, Dallas, & Gilmore.

Son of George Harton and brother of T.M. Harton, George Bruce Harton worked in the steel industry. Known throughout the city for his involvement in the steel industry, G. Bruce Harton was originally an employee of the Singer, Nimick & Company before it merged into the Crucible Steel Company. That company was linked closely with the Phoenix Iron Works of Phoenixville, Pennsylvania, which helped produce some of the first Ferris wheels manufactured after it appeared at the 1893 Chicago Columbian Exposition.

Ferris Wheel at Exposition Park (present day Point State Park)

Because Pittsburgh was a major player in the country's industrial revolution, it makes sense that companies such as Westinghouse Electric participated in the World's Columbian Exposition (commonly known as a World's Fair) in 1893, held in Chicago. A Pittsburgh resident and engineer, George Washington Gale Ferris Jr. designed and built what became known as the Ferris wheel for the fair. The original roundabout wheel (aka Ferris wheel) was patented and created by William Somers of Atlantic City, New Jersey. Ferris, who rode Somers' wheel in 1888, believed it would be a popular amusement ride, and so decided to design and erect his own.

With the excitement generated by the Ferris wheel in Chicago, the Phoenix Iron Works began building a 150-foot wheel for the city of Pittsburgh. This project led many people to believe the first Ferris wheel was in Pittsburgh, Pennsylvania; a fact that is simply incorrect. Among those who worked on the Phoenix wheel in Pittsburgh was Theodore Marshall Harton II, the son of T.M. Harton. Young Harton worked as a laborer to help erect the Phoenix wheel for the Pittsburgh Exposition. He even knew George Ferris and was fascinated by Ferris's wheel. The Pittsburgh Phoenix wheel was the younger Harton's introduction to the amusement industry and the Pittsburgh Exposition where he would operate his first amusements.

The Harton Family

Theodore Marshall and his wife, Emily (Rinehart), lived in Sharpsburg and had three children: Olive, Theodore Marshall II, and George Maurice II. The Rinehart family had long been associated with Pittsburgh as pioneers of the region. After the passing of T.M. Sr. in 1866, Emily remarried John Saint, a land agent for the Pittsburgh Bessemer & Lake Erie Railroad. This second marriage produced two half-siblings: sister Jessie Saint and Isa Grace. Isa passed away at the age of twelve.

George Maurice Harton II

George Maurice Harton II became a corporate attorney, admitted to the bar in December 1892. George worked primarily as a patent attorney. Graduating from Adrian College with a degree in philosophy, he later graduated from the University of Michigan with a law degree in 1892. In January 1893, he opened his own legal practice in Pittsburgh. His law practice became one of the largest in Western Pennsylvania, as he represented many businesses, including Republic Casualty Company, H.J. Heinz, and the T.M. Harton Company. Outside of his legal practice, he interested himself in manufacturing, and as president of the Augusta Venner Company, built a profitable business. The Harton brothers invested in a variety of businesses together, and being an attorney, George became his brother's closest advisor. George II married Carice Newman of Mechanicsburg, Ohio, and had two children: Ruth and George III.

Ruth was a talented tennis player and school student. According to Janet Von Twistern, her aunt was a self-taught violinist and pianist who performed in many piano concerts. Unfortunately, Ruth passed away at the young age of fourteen, leaving George III (seven) as an only child.

Olive Harton Jones, who had become wealthy in her own right, was known for her involvement in the local Pittsburgh community. She was actively involved with the Protestant Home for Incurables, a charitable institution that provided a home for citizens suffering from incurable diseases. Olive eventually married Colonel David Jones, a former chief engineer for the United States Navy. Jones is known as one of the fathers of modern engineering in the Navy. Because Olive never had children, she became close with half-sister Jessie's family. Jessie Saint married Charles Locey Beares Sr. in 1899. Charles Locey Beares II, born in 1902, became the first second generation Harton family member to work in

Switchback Railway
(present day Point State Park)

the amusement business started by his uncles. The Beares family was another pioneering family of Pittsburgh, involved in the iron and railroad industries. Charles Beares Sr.'s grandfather, Maj. Henry Beares, owned the first furniture store in Pittsburgh.

Prior to becoming involved in the amusement industry, Theodore Marshall Harton II—T.M., or Marsh, as he was known—worked as a produce commission merchant. Interestingly enough, T.M. and his family became close friends with Henry John (HJ) Heinz when he moved next to the Hartons and started his own business. At a young age, he lived an active life and always had the spirit for business and entrepreneurship. Entrepreneurship was not uncommon in Pittsburgh during this time, as the region played a key role in the country's Industrial Revolution. In 1893, Marsh established the T.M. Harton Company to build and operate Ferris wheels and various other amusement devices.

Establishing the Company

Originally told to give up on the harebrained idea of owning and operating an amusement device, Harton was promised a loan of $10,000, provided that he open a vegetable and produce stall in a market the Mellon family was building. Harton convinced the Mellon family to provide him the loan and

agreed to open the vegetable mart in addition to purchasing a carousel in 1893. The Mellons were surprised when the produce mart failed, and Harton paid off the loan from proceeds received from the carousel. According to Rudy Uzzell, an early amusement ride broker, the bankers did not know how Harton paid off the loan. Some were probably reluctant to believe the carousel produced a steady income. The truth was, the carousel at the Pittsburgh Exposition was an immediate success, and Harton found his calling. In 1895, Marsh began working with the James Griffith & Crane Scenic and Gravity Railroad Company as a salesman and ride concession operator. When the Greater Pittsburgh Exposition opened in 1895, Harton debuted the new Switchback Railway built by James Griffith & Crane. The attraction was built to meet the growing demand of the exposition crowds and Harton's own success as an amusement ride concessionaire. Harton spent $10,000 to construct the Switchback and charged patrons one nickel to ride.

Theodore Marshall Harton II was known as a progressive and modern businessman throughout his life. He had a wide range of interests and was devoted to the promotion of the welfare of his hometown. Harton, a conservative,

THE T. M. HARTON COMPANY

1115 Farmers Bank Bldg.,
PITTSBURG, PA.

Builders and Operators of Roller
Coasters, Scenic Railways, Carou-
sels and other Park Amusement
Devices.

We offer at low prices several
second-hand Carousels in excellent
condition.

Park Concessions Wanted.

was a member of the Pittsburgh Athletic Club and a devout lifelong Presbyterian. Everyone who knew him said his appearance and manners expressed his character, which, in turn, led to his own success and achievements.

Along with his brother George, the Harton brothers invested in outside companies to build an investment portfolio. One such company in which they invested money was the Randall Rotary Power Plug Company. This company manufactured and sold spark plugs for motorcycles and other vehicles.

Marsh Harton became well connected within the amusement industry rather quickly. He was a successful buyer, seller, and operator of amusement equipment. Ask anyone who works in the amusement industry and they will tell you the business is rather small and everyone is connected in one way or another. The same was said during the industry's early years. As technology advanced, the industry grew much faster.

The ability to recruit, cooperate, and network worked to T.M. Harton's benefit. He always wanted to associate with other individuals who were just as progressive. These relationships and partnerships would soon allow Harton to grow his amusement empire faster than any other company. Marsh also wanted members of his family to take on active and important roles within the company, which included his new brother-in-law, Charles Beares.

> "When he (Charles Beares Sr.) first married my grandmother (Jessie Saint Beares), T.M. was after him constantly to come work for the T.M. Harton Company. Eventually, T.M. convinced him to come work for him."
>
> *–Charles L. Beares III*

One of these early partnerships was with Lorenzo T. Yoder, who owned a building at 1235 Liberty Avenue in Pittsburgh, out of which Harton worked.

This building was home to Harton's produce business, which remained active until approximately 1902.

E. Joy Morris of Philadelphia, who is credited with designing and developing the more traditional Figure Eight Toboggan slide, sold Harton the rights to use his patent. The gentlemen entered into a contract to provide a new Figure Eight in 1901 for the Pittsburgh Exposition (current site of Point State Park). Harton owned and operated four attractions at the Pittsburgh Exposition: a Figure Eight roller coaster, a Ferris wheel, a carousel, and the Hippodrome, all except the Ferris Wheel operated until the conclusion of the 1916 exposition. The Hippodrome was an indoor vaudeville and moving picture theatre. The success of this venture provided opportunities for the company to add to the growing list of attractions for sale. Besides roller coasters and carousels, the company also built, operated, and sold fun houses (known as laughing galleries), Ferris wheels, old mill type rides, shooting gallery games, and movie theaters. The Figure Eight was built to replace the former Switchback Railway, which was lost in the Pittsburgh Exposition fire on St. Patrick's Day 1901. The success of these attractions helped to stimulate Harton's curiosity, which turned him into a successful owner and broker of amusement equipment.

Downtown Pittsburgh early 1900s

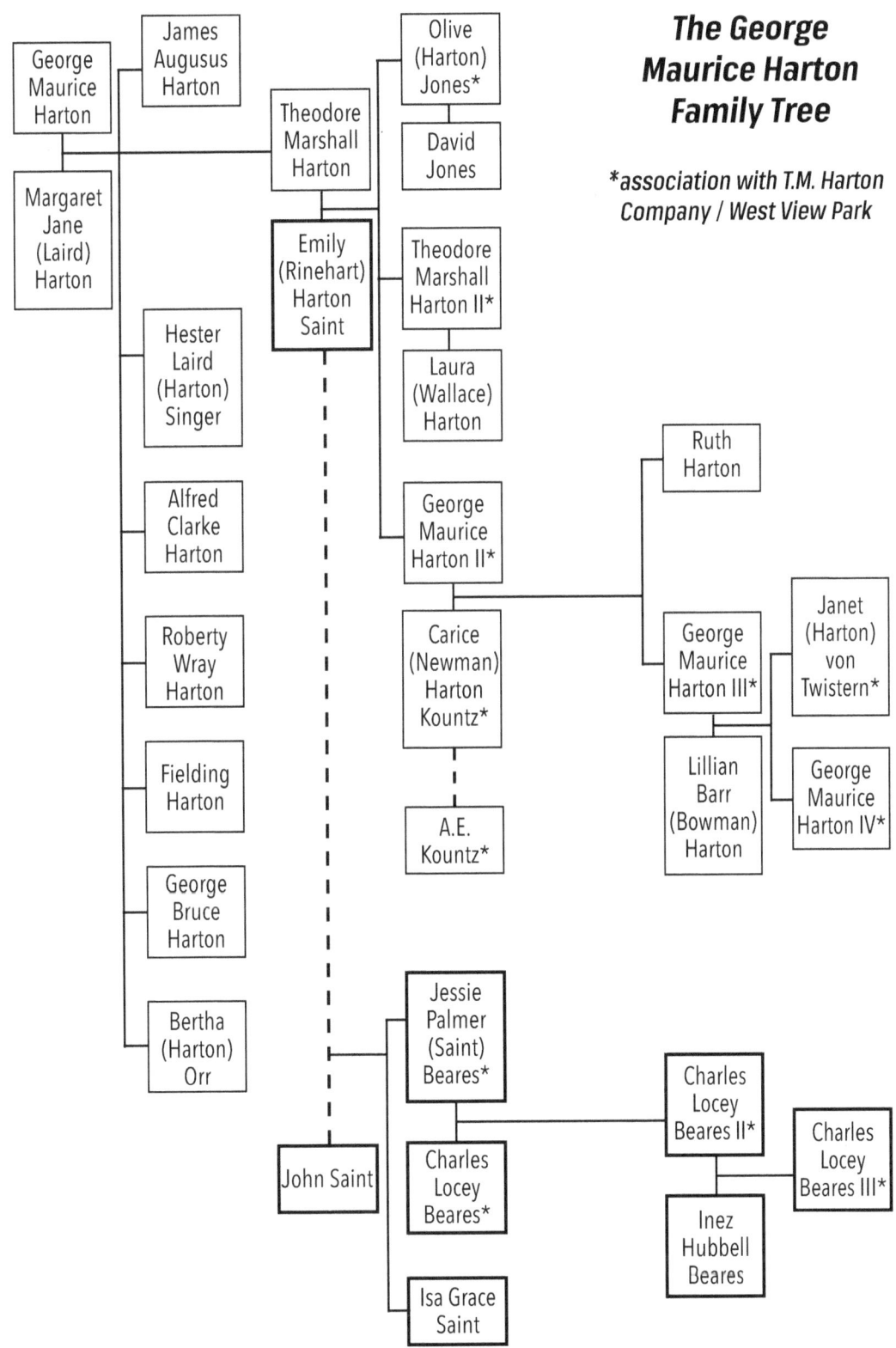

The George Maurice Harton Family Tree

*association with T.M. Harton Company / West View Park

Entrepreneur to Industry Leader

T.M. Harton positioned his company well enough to own and operate ride concessions at parks in other states. Harton loved to make money and saved as much as possible in order to provide funds for future amusement-related investments. He was financially savvy, paying cash for company investments and persuading investors outside of the amusement industry to support his efforts in growing his company. Harton, along with his brother George, were also well-rounded investors outside the amusement industry. These investments provided capital that assisted the T.M. Harton Company amusement concession business to grow to an amusement empire.

A concession owner would be contracted to operate his own equipment, in this case, an amusement ride, on a landowner's property. The concession owner would manage, maintain, and operate the attraction at the park and share a portion of the profit from the revenue generated with the land or park owner. The profitability, and later selling of these concessions by T.M. Harton, provided the much-needed cash reserve that enabled him to reinvest money into his own company. Depending on a ride's success and feasibility, park ownership could purchase the ride and assume full ownership from the concession owner operator. T.M Harton eventually formed multiple subsidiary companies for his ride concessions. In the early days of the amusement industry, this was common with all roller coasters, carousels, old mill type attractions, and games. Today, the concept still exists as revenue share partnerships, mainly for games, food, and/or rides that can easily be transported.

T.M. Harton Company subsidiary companies in 1901 and 1902 owned rides at parks such as Cedar Point (Sandusky, Ohio), Coney Island (Cincinnati, Ohio), Idlewild Park (Ligonier, Pennsylvania), Kennywood Park (West Mifflin, Pennsylvania), Pittsburgh Exposition (Pittsburgh, Pennsylvania), Conneaut Lake Park (Conneaut Lake, Pennsylvania), Waldameer Park (Erie,

Dip-The-Dips Coney Island Cincinnati, Ohio

Pennsylvania), Celeron Park (Jamestown, New York), Seabreeze Park (Rochester, New York), Idora Park (Youngstown, New York), Paxtang Park (Harrisburg, Pennsylvania), Olympic Park (Newark, New Jersey), and Eldridge Park (Elmira, New York).

With the growing popularity of the trolley park, T.M. Harton's goal was to own parks and not just rides. In time, the T.M. Harton Company owned controlling interest in Walbridge Park (Toledo, Ohio), Athletic Park (Buffalo, New York), and West View Park (Pittsburgh, Pennsylvania). In following his plan, Harton sought to obtain the necessary experience in operating a park before returning to Pittsburgh to start his own amusement park.

Walbridge & Athletic Park

Born on September 23, 1880, in Ligonier, Pennsylvania, Harry Franklin Covode was a page for the Pennsylvania House of Representatives and later in Washington, DC, during his youth. His grandfather, the Honorable John Covode of Greensburg, PA, had been a member of Congress for many years. Covode began his career in the amusement industry as a ride operator on a carousel located at Detroit's Riverview Park. Upon returning home, Covode found employment with T.M. Harton, helping erect a new carousel at Idlewild in 1899. Covode credited his time at Idlewild as the place where he received his first real training in the amusement industry. In 1917, the 1899 Carousel was replaced by an updated ride and new carousel building that remains in use today. A carousel built by the Philadelphia Toboggan Company later replaced Harton's carousel in 1931. Walbridge Park began in 1899 as a partnership with Idlewild Park carousel operator and T.M. Harton Company employee Harry F. Covode.

Prior to partnering with Covode, Harton established his presence in Toledo with the opening of amusement concessions nearby. The Walbridge Amusement Park Company officially opened on four and a half acres of leased property that featured a Griffith & Crane Scenic Figure Eight, a carousel, and an amusement game and free entertainment building called The Scenic. In the following years, Harton and Covode developed the property and removed The Scenic for a new Muller Brothers carousel and building and other amusements

Ye Old Mill at Walbridge Park

The Scenic at Walbridge Park

in 1906. Other new attractions included a dance pavilion, an old mill boat ride, frolic funhouse, and free concerts.

In 1905, six years after establishing Walbridge Park, the T.M. Harton Company purchased complete control of Athletic Park (later renamed Luna Park), in Buffalo, New York. T.M. Harton Company shareholder and manager of Luna Park, R.H. MacBroom, was appointed the new manager prior to the 1906 season and had this to say in the *Buffalo Morning Express* on April 19:

"It is our intention to establish Athletic Park on an entirely new basis and one that will be appreciated by the people of Buffalo and surrounding country."

T.M. Harton had made several early attempts to gain control of Athletic Park but only became successful in October 1905. Earlier in the year, Harton purchased the Figure Eight built by Fred Ingersoll at the park. Marsh also negotiated an option to purchase all other assets. Harton spent almost $7,000 erecting and installing a new carousel for the Athletic Park's grand opening in May 1904. The company invested $25,000 in park improvements for the 1906 season, including the purchase of additional acreage. Featured new attractions included a dance pavilion, a hippodrome, shoot-the-chutes, and bump-the-bump, while existing rides included the Figure Eight, a carousel, an old mill, and a circle swing. The significant investments by Harton and R.H. MacBroom, park manager, in 1906 continued, as another $75,000 would be spent for the 1907 season. The park, renamed Luna Park in 1907, saw the addition of multiple attractions. The

BUFFALO EVENING TIMES, MONDAY, OCTOBER 23, 1905.

ATHLETIC PARK IN NEW HANDS NOW

THE T. M. HARTON COMPANY OF PITTSBURG NOW IN CONTROL.

Athletic Park, the Main Street amusement resort, has changed hands. The T. M. Harton Company of Pittsburg, one of the largest concerns dealing in amusement devices in the country, has just finished negotiations with Robert F. Walter for the change of management.

Last summer T. M. Harton controlled the figure eight roller coaster at the park. He had made several previous attempts to control the entire park, but his efforts last summer were of no avail and the plan fell through. Now, however, he has come to an understanding with Mr. Walter and next summer the park will be under his management.

Many changes and improvements are contemplated by the T. M. Harton Company. George A. Lazear, one of the members of the company, yesterday announced that it was the intention of the company to spend fully $25,000 in the park before the 1906 season opens. It is assured that the park will be one of the finest places of amusement in the country when complete. New attractions, all of which will be elaborate, are to be added. The shows will be nothing but the best and no fake concessions will be allowed on the grounds.

Auto-Dip, or scenic railway, was erected at a cost of more than $25,000. T.M. Harton explained the investments in *The Buffalo Enquirer* of May 7, 1907:

"More money is being spent by the different companies than ever before. And I predict the biggest return for the amount invested by the amusement purveyor has ever known. Buffalo people will have just cause to be proud of its rejuvenated North Main Street park, for practically everything will be new and the park will be larger by two acres."

Figure Eight at Athletic Park

1908 saw the addition of the Tickler (similar to the one located in Coney Island) and improvements to the skating rink. While Harton and McBroom spent a great deal of money reinvesting in Luna Park, they were also interested in expanding business operations in New York. In 1908, the company won the contract to construct a large $20,000 roller coaster at Electric Park, in Kinderhook Lake, New York. The additions to Luna Park helped company profits grow, but a fire in the early morning of July 14, 1909, destroyed much of the park, creating a major setback to the progress made by Harton and McBroom. Harton sold Luna Park in 1909 because of the devastation left from the fire.

Conneaut Lake Park, Waldameer, & Ride Concessions

While trying to gain control of Athletic Park, the T.M. Harton Company continued to expand its ride businesses and introduced new concessions at Conneaut Lake Park, Waldameer Park, and Idora Park. 1905 saw the addition of a new carousel at Conneaut Lake Park. Supplying the new ride was the T.M. Harton Company, which had supplied the previous carousel they owned and

Conneaut Lake Park Carousel

Conneaut Lake Park Jack Rabbit

at the park since 1900. In 1914, a new carousel with horses and animals carved by Daniel and Alfred Muller of D.C. Muller Brothers, manufacturers of carousels, was installed at Conneaut Lake. T.M. Harton greatly appreciated the Mullers and ordered a large number of horses, figures, and decorative panels and frames for his carousels.

Over the years, the carousel at Conneaut Lake Park has been at the center of stories and speculation about the park and its future. Charlie Flynn, who in the 1980s and early part of the 1990s, owned Conneaut Lake Park, was roundly criticized when he sold off the original hand-carved horses from the ride. In order to retain the nostalgia of the ride without removing the entire ride, Flynn signed a contract with Carousel Works of Mansfield, Ohio, to carve exact replicas of the original horses. For most visitors outside the park and industry enthusiast groups, Conneaut's carousel horses have remained the same.

Conneaut Lake Park had an interesting history even during its early days. During the early days, numerous individuals and companies had invested in the company that owned the park. Conneaut Lake Park was struggling internally with the overhead cost of managing and maintaining park infrastructure. Unlike the other investors and partners, the T.M. Harton Company was extremely active in Conneaut Lake Park's development and ride concession business.

In 1905, a new carousel and building was also installed at Waldameer Park. The T.M. Harton Company also owned and operated a Figure Eight roller coaster at the park and built Waldameer's first fun house, House of Hilarity. Eventually, Waldameer purchased the carousel from the T.M. Harton Company, and then, in the 1980s, auctioned off its carousel animals to fund park expansion projects. The sales from the auction raised over $1 million dollars, which provided funds to start constructing a new water park, Water World.

T.M. Harton Co Carousel at Waldameer Park

A new carousel was later purchased and installed in the building designed and built by the T.M. Harton Company. Restored in the 1980s, the carousel building at Waldameer remains the oldest structure in the park.

Idora Park in Youngstown was also the home to a T.M. Harton-owned carousel, as was Luna Park in Cleveland. Both carousels were later replaced by a Philadelphia Toboggan Company standard model carousel. The Harton-designed carousel building remained at Idora Park until years after the park closed. Harton carousels also appeared at Rock Springs Park in Chester, West Virginia, and Paxtang Park in Harrisburg.

T.M. Harton Company built and owned the Carousel and Figure Eight at Rock Springs Park

A T.M. Harton Carousel is shown to the far left in this photo at Paxtang Park

Growth of the T.M. Harton Company was in large part due to acquiring ownership in amusement parks and growing the ride business. Marsh realized he needed to expand his concession offerings and realized the film business offered that opportunity.

Harton Theater Company

With the 1905 opening of the nation's first Nickelodeon theater dedicated to moving pictures in Pittsburgh, T.M. Harton quickly realized the concept had much potential. The T.M. Harton Company entered the film business in 1906 while operating the Hippodrome at the Pittsburgh Exposition. In conjunction with opening the Regent Theater in Elmira, New York, in September 1915, a new subsidiary company, the Harton Theater Company was incorporated. T.M. Harton Company funded construction and owned the theater. Marsh Harton realized the success of the movie theater would rely not only on the appearance and design of the theater but, more importantly, on projection and lighting, to provide the best quality picture. The business

Harton Theater Company Incorporated At $50,000

Certificate Is Filed in Albany in Connection With New Theater Deal for Elmira— Two Pittsburghers and One New Yorker Directors

Albany, Jan. 19.—(Special.)—A certificate of incorporation has been filed with the Secretary of State by the Harton Theater Company, of Elmira. The capital stock is $50,000, consisting of shares of $100 each, and the directors for the first year are as follows: E. C. Berger and F. M. Harton, of Pittsburgh, and John McLaren, of New York City.

This is the company which will build and operate the proposed new theater at Water street and Railroad avenue. It was announced by a representative of the company before leaving the city that the company would be incorporated at $100,000.

The final plans for the theater now are being perfected and will be here in about a week when bids will be asked. The capital is entirely that of the T. M. Harton Company, large theatrical and amusement promoters of Pittsburgh. The construction and contract work is to be let to local contractors.

Atlantic City Coaster

remained profitable for many years, and the Harton Theater Company would own and manage a number of other theaters. While the theater company provided a boost in T.M. Harton Company profits for the next decade, it did not become the dominant division.

Pittsburgh is Home

During the early part of the 1900s, roller coasters were being built in and around every major city in the United States. Roller coasters, or as they were called at the time, toboggans, were commonly found at parks, fairs, and other similar entertainment sites. When the amusement park boom occurred, meaning when many parks started opening up, individuals from Pittsburgh played a huge role in shaping the foundation of the amusement industry. During these early years, the T.M. Harton Company became one of leading companies building side-friction Figure Eight Toboggan coasters and scenic railways. Pittsburgh had become one of the premier locations to enter the amusement industry. Along with T.M. Harton, notable industry pioneers such as A.S. McSwigan, F.W. Henninger, Joe and Al McKee, and Josiah, Eugene, and Fred Pearce were all from Pittsburgh. The amusement industry has always been relatively small, meaning managers have always been well connected. As these individuals launched successful careers, they attracted others, including those in their families, to join them. These families often started the making of multi-generational family businesses. Fred and LeForest Ingersoll, who weren't from Pittsburgh, moved their homes there because of the city's industrial and labor market.

Like Harton, Fred Ingersoll was another early amusement industry pioneer and innovator, who built many early Figure Eight side-friction roller coasters. He is also credited with building and creating the modern-day amusement park concept and chain, as Ingersoll owned and operated Luna parks in multiple cities. From 1905–1909, Ingersoll owned and operated Luna Park in Pittsburgh's Oakland neighborhood.

Joe McKee worked for Fred Ingersoll at Pittsburgh's Luna Park,

Fred Pearce with his father, Josiah

managing the park's theater and later building structures and coasters as a carpenter throughout the country.

McKee was selected to help construct Ingersoll's Luna parks throughout America and Mexico. It was through this relationship that McKee would work hand in hand with Ingersoll's chief engineer, John A. Miller, on constructing and managing a number of his early rides. In addition, Charles Paige and Vernon Keenan began their careers at Ingersoll Engineering, working directly with and under John Miller. Ingersoll's work also attracted the interest of two brothers originally from Sandusky, Ohio.

The Vettel Family

Erwin Vettel, the oldest of nine children born to Andreas (Andrew) and Anna Vettel in 1878, came to the United States with his parents from Germany in 1880. The family consisted of five boys and four girls: Erwin, Elsie, Catharina, Louis, Edward, Anna, Andrew, John "Jack," and Lydia. Three of the sons, Erwin, Edward (born 1885), and Andrew (born 1887) all pursued successful careers within the amusement industry designing and constructing roller coasters.

Erwin Vettel

According to Erwin's son Andrew in a May 19, 1968, article in the *Pittsburgh Press*, his father's first coaster job was at Cedar Point in Sandusky, where the Vettel Family called home. Prior to working in construction projects with the amusement industry, Erwin, who was educated in Sandusky, was engaged in contracting and construction work. He was a civil and construction engineer and started in the trade in 1898.

During their youth on Lake Erie, brothers Erwin and Edward designed and sold a gravity method of moving ice on the lake to the neighboring icehouses. It was at Cedar Point where Erwin started in amusement park construction, eventually recruiting his brother to join him.

The Vettels were attracted to Pittsburgh because the amusement industry was thriving there. The first project they worked on with Theodore Harton and the T.M. Harton Company was in Canada, at the annual Canadian National Exposition (CNE) in Toronto, building the Scenic Auto-Dip, which operated between 1902 and 1906. The large ride, built, designed, and operated by the T.M. Harton Company, cost 15 cents per ride or 25 cents for two riders.

The Scenic Auto Dip at the National Exposition in Toronto

Constuction of Toronto's Scenic Auto Dip

After the project at the CNE, Harton retained the Vettels as regular employees for his company's many projects. Harton knew that with the growing demand of projects, he needed engineers on staff. In 1905, the Vettel brothers moved from Sandusky to start construction on Harton coasters elsewhere. The increased work and responsibility provided by T.M. Harton led Erwin Vettel to stop working for Fred Ingersoll while continuing to work with his fellow engineers and builders. The Vettel and Harton relationship played an important role in obtaining ride concessionaire business at Cedar Point, a park in which the Vettels previously completed work for Ingersoll. In 1906, Harton installed one of the first carousels at the resort, costing $10,000, and billed as the finest ever constructed. The carousel started a successful relationship between the T.M. Harton Company and Cedar Point management. The carousel operated until 1945, when Cedar Point replaced the ride with a Dentzel carousel that still operates at the park today. The building stood at the front of the park on what is known as the Million Dollar Midway until 1993.

With Erwin and Edward now designing and building coasters for the T.M. Harton Company, the Ingersoll Construction Company faced a strong competitor working out of the same market. Prior to his involvement with

T.M. Harton, Erwin was under contract as a construction engineer for Fred Ingersoll's early Figure Eight coasters or toboggans. Ingersoll's company built Figure Eight Toboggans at many parks, such as Kennywood, Conneaut Lake, Idora Park in Ohio, and Seabreeze in New York. Andrew Vettel said in a 1968 *Pittsburgh Press* newspaper article:

> "Dad trained carpenters especially for the work. And often one of them would be hired to stay and take care of a ride after it had been built. Probably 20 of his assistants took over jobs that way. Charles Mach stayed at Kennywood after the first one they built here. The family built over 100 in all—all over North and South America and Europe."

The Vettel brothers began to play a vital role in the expansion of the T.M. Harton Company and the construction of roller coasters owned by the company. In a relatively short period of time, the T.M. Harton Company experienced an increase in ride concessions thanks to the work of Erwin and Ed Vettel. Pittsburgh became the roller coaster capital of the world, and the city became the training and recruiting location for future roller coaster builders, designers, and experts. The popularity of the modern-day roller coaster was growing and it would soon become an international phenomenon, helping grow the amusement park industry.

T.M. Harton Company built the Waldameer Carousel Pavilion

The T.M. Harton Company owned and operated a Figure Eight, Carousel, and funhouse at Waldameer

The T.M. Harton Company, built, owned, and operated a Figure Eight and Carousel at Oakford Park in Greensburg, PA

Chapter 3

Industry Leader with a Global Footprint

The Global Footprint

With the growing popularity of the roller coaster in the United States, by 1907, the craze moved to Europe and became a global success. Theodore Harton led the way by erecting the first toboggan slide or modern-day roller coaster at White City Park, located in Manchester, England, in 1907. G.A. Lazear, a partner in the T.M. Harton Company, oversaw construction and early operation of the ride in its infancy stage. According to a cablegram from Lazear to T.M. Harton in Pittsburgh, the ride brought in about $2,500 in the first six days of operation. The English were quick to enjoy the new experience and, as Lazear believed, the next years would lead to more parks contracting with the T.M. Harton Company to build more roller coasters. Excited that the newest sensation was met with immediate success, Harton was eager to meet the growing demand.

Shortly after the cablegram from Lazaer, Theodore Harton traveled regularly to Europe to check on the progress of his coaster projects. To keep up with the dynamic demand and global interest in roller coasters, Harton signed a contract with the James Griffith & Crane Scenic and Gravity Railway

Company to construct several new roller coasters to be owned and operated by the T.M. Harton Company. T.M. Harton also partnered with Josiah Pearce to finance the construction of new roller coasters designed by John A. Miller.

Miller, who is considered the father of the modern-day roller coaster, held numerous patents that modern-day roller coasters still use. Fred Ingersoll saw the potential in Miller, and hired him between 1904–1905 to design what would be considered non-traditional toboggans. Because Miller began designing non-traditional roller coasters, the T.M. Harton Company began doing the same in 1910 at the request of President T.M. Harton. Just as Harton saw the potential in the European market, he saw the great potential in this new design concept.

Strategic Engineering Masters - The Vettels

As demand and opportunity for roller coaster concessions increased, T.M. Harton recognized he needed to hire at least one engineer to grow his company. By hiring Erwin and Edward (Ed) Vettel as engineers, Harton had two key individuals who'd transform the company into a dominant position within the amusement industry. The hiring of the Vettels also opened the door for additional partnerships and career opportunities.

In 1907, the Vettels built the first of multiple roller coasters the T.M. Harton Company owned at Coney Island

Stella and Edward Vettel, Sr.

The Harton Carousel at Coney Island

in Cincinnati. When Coney Island management wanted Harton to install another roller coaster, he also negotiated rights to the carousel concession. Edward Vettel, was not as fond of traveling as his brother and became heavily involved in overseeing domestic projects, including the construction and operation of West View Park. Although he worked primarily at West View, Ed still traveled occasionally to design and construct rides, most of which were financed by the T.M. Harton Company. Not only did Ed design roller coasters, he also designed and constructed the park's buildings. The Vettels oversaw the construction crew that built each new ride. While Ed remained at West View Park, Erwin traveled internationally for the T.M. Harton Company. Simultaneously, the Vettels were responsible for developing a strong reputation for the T.M. Harton Company both domestically in North America and internationally. The Vettel brothers would also be strategically establishing the groundwork for multiple generational company leadership.

> "They were both engineers. None of us know if they ever designed any coasters together on a single project. They were in different parts of the world working for the T.M. Harton Company."
>
> -Kathy Vettel Hilton

By 1910, the T.M. Harton Company had built more than forty roller coasters in the United States and by 1915, forty-three in Europe. The company was one of the first amusement businesses to use the same ride design to replicate at multiple locations, similar to that of an assembly line pioneered during the Industrial Revolution. Harton's ambition and support pushed Erwin Vettel continually to seek new opportunities and new markets to expand the company's footprint in Europe. According to Erwin's son Andrew, who became known for his affiliation at Kennywood, his father was overseas 80 percent of the time between 1906 and 1929. Erwin also built roller coasters designed by John Miller, including those owned by the T.M. Harton Company and Pearce family, as well as the Big Dipper at Blackpool Pleasure Beach in England. In addition to multiple roller coasters in England, the T.M Harton Company

Erwin Vettel (far right) and crew sit proudly in a soon to be commissioned ride vehicle in Europe

built rides in Germany, France, Belgium, and Hungary. Erwin's grandson, also named Erwin, explained:

> "My grandfather Erwin didn't mind traveling on a boat. Ed was uneasy traveling on a boat so he stayed in Pittsburgh. Being that my grandfather was born in Germany, he was bilingual in German and English, which made it easier for him to travel overseas for T.M. Harton."

In 1911, Andrew Vettel followed in his older brothers' footsteps into the roller coaster construction business and working for the T.M. Harton Company. Erwin taught his younger brother the skills of the trade, skills he would put to use after establishing himself and his own construction company. In order to differentiate himself from his brothers, Andrew started spelling his last name as Vettal. While he spent a little more than eleven years of his younger life in Europe, working with his brother Erwin, Andrew maintained a residence in England as well as Springfield, Ohio. In 1946, Andrew returned to his hometown of Sandusky to supervise the reconstruction of the Cyclone at Cedar Point.

Erwin and Edwards brother Andrew, stands (far left) with three other members of the construction team

T.M. Harton Company roller coaster construction as seen in Europe

T.M. Harton Company construction crew in Europe

Figure Eight construction in England circa 1910

Giant Racer, Pleasure Park, Redcar England

Figure 8 Bahn Munich German circa 1909

In 1913, Rudy and Frank Uzzell joined Erwin Vettel as partners in England to erect rides for the T.M. Harton Company in order to sustain growth. Rudy would go on to become a prominent ride distributor and salesman of amusement park services. A former colleague of Harry Traver, Uzzell later formed the R.S. Uzzell Corporation, which billed itself as the leader in used rides specializing in rebuilding and reconditioning, as well as the largest exporters of amusement park equipment. Uzzell also became one of the industry's earliest historians.

Strategic Partnerships

Harton capitalized on the financial mishaps of Fred Ingersoll. The T.M. Harton Company changed with the times, updating rides as well as buying and/or constructing new equipment. T.M. Harton was a successful businessman who established ride concessions at various parks, building new and purchasing existing attractions, some originally built by the Ingersoll Engineering & Construction Company. While Harton retained long-term ownership in select locations, he typically sold off many of the rides his company constructed after proving years of profitability and return on investment.

By 1912, the ownership and management of the Ingersoll Engineering & Construction Company changed hands. Fred Ingersoll left the company and was succeeded by his business partner, Elwood Salsbury. Through Ingersoll, Salsbury formed a coaster business with John Miller, known as the Miller & Salsbury Partnership. This partnership later incorporated as the John A. Miller Company in 1923.

While Salsbury changed the business model for the company, John Miller went on to design rides for Miller & Salsbury, Josiah Pearce & Sons, Philadelphia Toboggan Company, Miller & Baker, and other companies. Salsbury managed the company from New York City until 1918, when he and T.M. Harton purchased all of its remaining assets, which were then operated by Harton and Salsbury. Interestingly enough, Harton obtained ownership in cross-town competition's Kennywood Racing Coaster Company. This company owned and operated the Racer roller coaster, which John Miller designed for Ingersoll Engineering in 1910. The coaster remained in operation at Kennywood until 1926.

The T.M. Harton Company pushed forward in selling and constructing new roller coasters at a rapid pace. Over the years, the Pearce family and the Harton Company built and constructed rides such as Trip Thru the Clouds at Milford Stern's Riverview Park, the Scenic Railway at Blue Grass Park, and the Derby Racer at Revere Beach. With the development of the roller coaster, Figure Eight-style rides began to disappear in favor of the out and back concept that started to appear around 1910. The Harton and Pearce relationship worked as a partnership, as the T.M. Harton Company were part owners of the Josiah Pearce & Sons Company, and Josiah Pearce was a partner in various subsidiary companies controlled by Harton.

Miller designed numerous coasters that the Pearce family operated as concessions. Fred W. Pearce purchased the Trip Thru the Clouds roller coaster in Detroit for $5,000 and made a profit of $100,000 in the first season of ownership. The Pearce family, natives of Pittsburgh, started in the amusement business as some of the earliest builders and managers of amusement attractions at Conneaut Lake Park. Pearce's father, Josiah, a builder of marine engines, owned and operated a steamboat on Conneaut Lake in 1903. Two years later, the Pearce family built and managed an old mill boat ride owned by the 20th Century Amusement Company. Fred Pearce, who was seventeen when entering the amusement industry, branched out into coaster construction and park operations. In large part, with help from the T.M. Harton Company, the Pearce family became successful pioneers in the amusement industry as park owners and concession operators. Fred Pearce is best known as the innovator who first used treated lumber in roller coaster construction. Pearce would go on to build and own Walled Lake Park near Detroit, Excelsior Amusement Park in Excelsior, Minnesota, and become president of the National Association of Amusement Parks, Pools, and Beaches (NAAPPB).

As John Miller moved on to other projects from the Harton & Pearce partnership, a young Vernon Keenan found work as a construction engineer for the Pearce family. Keenan, who was influenced by these early designers and builders, went on to have a successful career in the amusement industry as a roller coaster designer, most notably with Harry Baker and the National Amusement Device Company. Keenan is best known for designing the Coney Island Cyclone, located in Coney Island, in Brooklyn, New York.

Key Innovations

In 1913, while working as a carpenter in New York, a young immigrant from Romania named Aurel Vaszin was offered an opportunity by John Miller to go to New Haven, Connecticut, where the Ingersoll Engineering Company was erecting a racing coaster. By the fall, Vaszin traveled to Lakeside Park in Dayton, Ohio, and then worked with Fred Pearce on a roller coaster in Detroit, Michigan. In 1918, Vaszin secured his first contract to build roller coaster cars for Kennywood in Pittsburgh. This opportunity led to the formation of the Dayton Funhouse and Riding Device Company in 1919. Eventually, the company changed its name to National Amusement Device Company or NAD. Through Vaszin's involvement with the Ingersoll Engineering Company, which was later owned by the T.M. Harton Company, Ed Vettel found an opportunity to go into business for himself and be a contracted designer/engineer for the roller coaster manufacturer. Vettel designed and consulted on multiple coasters for Vaszin's company.

In 1914, the T.M. Harton Company secured a contract to build and operate a roller coaster concession at Idora Park in Youngstown, Ohio. Ed Vettel designed the new out and back Dip the Dips roller coaster. After an accident where two roller coaster trains collided, T.M. Harton traveled to Youngstown to evaluate the safety devices on the attraction. Knowing it was important to take prompt corrective action and evaluate safety measures, Harton developed a unique check and balance system with Ed Vettel that would aid ride operators. When the Dip the Dips reopened, the safety system installed informed station operators where each train was on the course of the track. This allowed for a smooth ride and avoided further risk of trains colliding. This became one of the first examples, if not the first example, of an early blocking system used on a roller coaster, something that is currently used on roller coasters around the world. A light board using this concept was installed and used on the West View Park Dips, Conneaut Lake Park Blue Streak, and Lakeside Amusement Park Cyclone in Denver, Colorado. The light board for each ride also featured a painting of the attraction, with artwork by Ed Vettel.

Although the new safety system proved to be a success, ridership on the Dip the Dips declined. Due to the decline in ridership, Ed Vettel and the T.M. Harton Company returned to Idora Park in 1924 to design and construct a

Dip The Dips, Cleethropes, England

new roller coaster using under friction wheel technology. John Miller developed the underfriction wheel, or upstop wheel, in 1919. This new development allowed roller coaster designers to incorporate steeper drops and sharper curves into their ride designs. The patent consisted of wheels that ran under the track to keep the roller coaster car from leaving the track. Ed Vettel used this patent to his advantage when designing the Idora Park Jack Rabbit in future roller coasters. The new Jack Rabbit replaced the Dip the Dips and remained in operation until Idora Park ceased operations following the 1984 summer season.

For the rest of the 1910s, Theodore Harton established himself as one of the premier leaders in the industry. Not only was he held in high regard because of his understanding of the operational logistics of the business, he was also respected for who he was as a person. Those who became employed by Harton became loyal and looked up to him as a mentor. Hired in 1906 by Harton himself, Walter Williams became a long-term employee who monitored the company's finances. Eventually, Williams was promoted to the secretary-treasurer of the T.M. Harton Company.

The Glen Island Dips

"In the summertime, Marsh had my grandfather (Charles Beares), grand-mother (Jessie Beares), and father, who was born by then, go to various parks around the country, where he (T.M. Harton) had concessions. He'd have my grandfather run those concessions. He spent time in Atlantic City on a roller coaster the T.M. Harton Company owned and spent two years at a park in Albany, NY, where they owned a carousel and Figure Eight. Then they went to Conneaut Lake Park in 1906."

- Charles Beares III

In 1906, the T.M. Harton Company owned and operated carousels and tobog-gan slides in twenty-five different domestic parks, and by 1910, over forty. In less than a decade, the T.M. Harton Company had become one of the largest amusement enterprises in the world; some individuals outside the organiza-tion claimed it to be the largest. The company owned and operated rides in al-most every part of the northeast United States, and by 1915, it had forty-three different locations of rides in Europe.

As the Harton empire grew and profits soared, T.M. Harton began look-ing for an area to build a park in the Pittsburgh region to anchor the company assets. By establishing offices at a locally-owned amusement park, Harton knew he could concentrate on further expanding his company's footprint.

Establishing a new home park would also provide the opportunity to showcase rides and roller coasters designed and built by the company. The goal was to always keep Pittsburgh at the heart of the business and home for the company headquarters. Knowing that Kennywood was the strongest amusement park on the east side of the city, Harton knew he needed to secure a location on the opposite side of the city in a potentially up and coming area.

The Idora Park Jack Rabbit, and the sign that proudly hung in the station

Revere Beach Derby Racer

Arriving to the finish line on the Revere Beach Derby Racer.

T.M. Harton crew standing on the lift hill of
one of their new toboggans in Europe

Establishing a Home Base 'West View Park'

The story of West View Park starts in 1904 before the installation of amusement ride equipment. The land on which West View Park stood was originally a community park, where a lake, picnic pavilions, and a dance pavilion stood for public use. At the time, and on the weekends, Pittsburghers typically escaped the city to get away from the smog of the industrial businesses and to enjoy simple recreation.

The name West View Park derives from the name of the West View neighborhood. It is said that the West View name came from pioneers who traveled north from the city of Pittsburgh. These early pioneers, who settled in what is now called the North Hills neighborhood of Pittsburgh, appreciated the glorious view to the west as they traveled the Venango Trail.

For seventy-one years, most patrons traveled to the West View Park amusement park via Route 19, better known as Perry Highway. Perry Highway was a heavily traveled route by horse and wagon. Due to the region's hilly terrain, the road needed to be expanded on multiple occasions. Reconfiguration of the road led to the creation of the famous Horseshoe Bend. This new road allowed wagons to maneuver the steep grade more easily. By the late

1890s, two oil well discoveries next to Horseshoe Bend led to an influx of new settlers and business to the area. Today, a small portion of the once grand Perry Highway remains, and the section that still exists passes the former site of one of the nation's most popular and memorable amusement parks.

By the early 1900s, the Allegheny-Bellevue Land Company had the Freehold Real Estate Company acquire hillside and farmlands that had been part of the large tracts of land owned by the earliest known families in the area: the Reel, Hiland-Collin, Scott, and Robinson families. As part of the Freehold Real Estate Company plan, the neighborhood would be supported by new public transportation: a trolley system.

PARKS

Pleasure Resorts
Summer Gardens

NEW PARK FOR PITTSBURG

West View Park is the name of what will next spring be Pittsburg's newest amusement resort. Three hundred thousand dollars are to be spent on thirty acres of land on the outskirts of Allegheny and Pittsburg, and with all the amusement devices known to the summer park promoter West View Park will next spring and summer bid heavily for public patronage.

The West View Park Co., headed by T. M. Harton and F. W. Henninger, has leased a site for a period of ten years and has applied for a charter. Work began last week. A semi-natural lake of considerable dimensions adds to the attractiveness of the place, and the land is covered with beautiful shade trees. The site is said to be naturally adapted for park purposes and will need very little work to put it in readiness for the installation of devices. It is probable that next winter the lake will be used for skating purposes.

Most of the concessions will be owned by the operators of the park who now control large concessions in many parks throughout the country. T. M. Harton, who is to be president of the company, is a Pittsburger, and is well known to the amusement business. F. W. Henninger, to be secretary and treasurer, has been in the business for a number of years.

The promoters claim for the new resort that it can be reached from both Pittsburg and Allegheny for a five cent fare. Special arrangements will be made with the traction company, which, though not financially interested directly, will co-operate in every way with the management of the new resort.

Traveling back to the city of Pittsburgh became much easier for those living in the newly created West View Borough, which was formally established in 1905. West View Park as a proper name came after 1905. The trolley companies typically popularized and rejuvenated preexisting recreation retreats for city folk during the industrial revolution.

T.M. Harton knew owning and operating his own park would allow for greater business opportunities and income. The opportunity to own a park in his hometown presented itself in 1905, and on December 2, 1905, he settled on a ten-year agreement with the Freehold Real Estate Company to lease thirty acres of property located in the North Hills. Organized as the West View Park Company, it announced plans to spend $300,000 on the new park and open in the summer of 1906.

To raise capital for the project, stock was sold to interested individuals willing to invest in the new company. The original lake, which was 150 feet wide and 1,200 feet long was slightly altered and used for the Mystic Chutes attraction. Construction on the semi-natural lake started shortly after the

George Maurice Harton II

T.M. Harton II

lease agreement was signed. The property adjoining the then called West View or Bellmere Lake, was leased for $3,000 per year. The enlarged five-acre lake was renamed Lake Placid. The lake was connected to a creek that ran close in proximity to the Ross Township line, adjacent to the property and through the borough of West View.

During the early years of amusement parks, it was uncommon for park management to own the land on which amusements were built or placed. Typically, a separate company such as a railroad company owned the land and park. The location of the new West View Park was ideal, as the streetcar line made a loop on what is now Route 19 (Perry Highway) to return to the city of Pittsburgh for a five-cent fare.

While streetcar or railway companies built many early amusement parks, West View Park was entirely financed by T.M. Harton and his companies. The location (two miles north of the city limits) made business sense, based on new and existing infrastructure and the influx of settlers to the area. The local community population grew over the years, which provided the park with many nearby patrons. The park and its location also provided an escape for individuals living closer to Pittsburgh, where manufacturing and labor-intensive jobs filled the sky with smoke and soot from the mills. West View was located far enough away from the city that the air was much cleaner and healthier to breathe.

Signing the agreement to erect an amusement park in West View were T.M. Harton, his brother, George M. Harton, and F.W. Henninger. On March 3, 1906, the *Harrisburg Telegraph* reported that the Commonwealth of Pennsylvania State Department had chartered twenty-two new corporations. At the bottom of the list was a company valued at $100,000: West View Park Company, Pittsburg. This was during the time Pittsburgh spelled the city's name without the ending "h." Without hesitation, Harton asked many of his close friends and existing partners to invest in his latest project. Several days later, stockholders of the West View Park Company elected its officers. T.M. Harton was named president, O.C. MacKalip vice president, and F.W. Henninger secretary and treasurer. The first board of directors were T.M. Harton, W.D. Johnston, E.D. Comstock, O.C. MacKalip, E.C. Berger, and F.W. Henninger.

Oliver MacKalip, who previously operated the T.M. Harton Company carousel at Idlewild was named West View Park's first general manager. Of everyone on the board of directors, Fred Henninger is probably the most recognizable name due to his affiliation with Andrew S. McSwigan and Kennywood Park in West Mifflin. These two families have been associated with Kennywood since its early days. Another original partner in West View Park was A.E. Meagan. Meagan eventually left the West View Park Company to join McSwigan and Henninger at Kennywood. While Henninger and Meagan sold their interest in the West View Park Company, McSwigan did not elect to sell his ownership until years later. McSwigan was eventually elected to the West View Park Company Board of Directors.

Henninger, a lumber salesman, made his way into the business selling lumber

Andrew S. McSwigan

for roller coasters and financing the projects. His working relationship with Fred Ingersoll and T.M. Harton took him to Conneaut Lake Park, where Henninger was secretary for the Conneaut Lake Park Company. Henninger later married the daughter of E.D. Comstock, the first general manager of Conneaut Lake Park. Comstock worked at Conneaut Lake Park and also became involved in the operations at West View Park and Kennywood because of his relationship with Fred Henninger. Comstock remained involved in the West View Park Company for years and became an active stockholder and director. He was also instrumental in determining which attractions should debut at the park.

As he later did for Kennywood, Comstock encouraged parks to purchase insurance, which he sold to them. It was a wise investment for the T.M. Harton Company to purchase fire and casualty insurance in the early years, and the long-term impact on this early decision would help the company years later. F.W. Henninger wrote during a West View Park Company stockholder meeting on March 16, 1906:

"E.D. Comstock moved that the president be instructed to place immediately fire insurance protection on all the buildings of the company."

Concept art for West View Park (1906)

The original administration office under construction - April 29, 1906

Welcome to West View Park

West View Park officially opened as an amusement park on Wednesday, May 23, 1906, with Danny Nirella's Fourteenth Regiment Band performing in the dance pavilion. The park opened with three amusement rides: Mystic Chute, a combination Shoot-the-Chute and boat ride, a carousel, and the Figure Eight roller coaster. The first season at West View Park proved very successful.

The new park also offered a variety of additional attractions, including an arcade and photograph gallery, rowboats, ponies and burros for children, and Hale's Tour of the World, a moving picture panorama. Hale's Tour of the World was the precursor of the modern-day 4D movie theater experience. In its day, Hale's Tour of the World theatres were replicas of railroad passenger cars, complete with a variety of real-life sound effects. Hale's Tour of the World was extremely popular in the early 1900s, with over 200 units located in large cities and parks, while 150 units were located in smaller cities.

Prior to the 1907 summer season, F.W. Henninger resigned from his position as secretary-treasurer of West View Park Company because he accepted the secretary-treasurer position with the Kennywood Park Corporation, which had just been chartered. Walter Williams filled the position of secretary-treasurer of the West View Park Company.

Frederick W. Henninger

Members of the Harton family have stated that F.W. Henninger left the West View Park Company after the first operating season because he and T.M. Harton did not share the same vision for the park. In the very early days, West View Park catered more toward entertainment, attractions, and keeping the landscape of the property true to its original look. Additionally, Harton encouraged all guests to bring their own meals and utilize the shelters on site. Bill Henninger, grandson of F.W. Henninger explained:

> "It's hard to tell why FWH left West View, but there very well may have been some personality and power issues. I suspect, however, the overriding reason Henninger left was because he wanted to cut his own path and recognized the unbridled potential at Kennywood, with its size and the booming demographics throughout the Mon Valley."

Original West View Park Company Letterhead

On the Pike, West View Park, North Side, Pittsburgh, Pa.

The Mystic Chute was one of the parks original rides

T.M. Harton had a laid-back approach on how he envisioned people would spend money at the park. Because Harton and Henninger began to have different visions, Henninger left to join Andrew McSwigan at Kennywood because he agreed with McSwigan's business model. While the two gentlemen and families were no longer business partners, they remained friends. Although Henninger moved on, West View Park management prepared new rides and attractions for the 1907 season. New attractions for 1907 included a Katzenjammer Castle funhouse and Razzle Dazzle. Early funhouses featured dark, narrow halls and passageways, staircases, and moving, springing, and suspended floors. Katzenjammer Castle funhouses featured humorous scenes with animals, ghouls, noises, air jets, and slides.

For much of its history, West View Park maintained the original layout as designed by E.L. Currier. Over the years, changes occurred to the midways, such as expansions, but in the end, West View would remain a one midway park. The property's original picnic pavilions attracted schools, churches, and families to hold picnics during the inaugural season in 1906. The very first school picnic held at the park was the West Homestead Public Schools on May 26. Schools from as far away as Wilkinsburg held picnics at West View Park. Amusement parks were typically established on property already in use for recreation.

Early 1900s view of the main midway

The park's original Penny Arcade

T.M. Harton incorporated existing picnic pavilion and picnic areas into his new home park layout. Tables continued to be provided under the trees, allowing families to bring food or picnic baskets to enjoy the day. Similar to admission, the tables were free to guests, as were

One of the park's original dining pavilions

tables in the large dining pavilion. Guests who preferred not to bring a basket could purchase a meal at a reasonable price in a pavilion dubbed The Casino.

Offices for the West View Park Company and parent company, T.M. Harton Company, remained located in the Farmers Bank Building in downtown Pittsburgh. One feature of West View Park that never changed from Harton's initial investment was the bridge located inside the park's streetcar entrance

The park's original Band Stage. The Figure Eight roller coaster loading station is at the far right

that connected both hills. Park guests could utilize this bridge to walk from the dance pavilion to the athletic field and picnic pavilions without walking up and down hills.

West View Park became the site of large gatherings, which then grew into annual picnics and repeat patrons. Vaudeville acts, orchestras, and concert and military bands performed weekly at the park as entertainment to attract crowds. For years, the park hosted church groups, especially those from the Pittsburgh Catholic Diocese. During picnics, events were held at the athletic field and water sports on Lake Placid. Group picnics took advantage of the sporting, boating, swimming, running, free band concerts, and dancing available at West View. This recreational use reflects how people used picnic parks before modern amusement rides.

T.M. Harton set his eyes on the continued success of West View Park and the amusement industry. In keeping with his vision for the park, he strived to keep a balance of free entertainment options and pay-to-ride amusement attractions. The Figure Eight was enlarged and rebuilt for the 1909 season. Although Harton had his brother-in-law, Charles Beares, travel during the operating season to inspect T.M. Harton Company assets, he spent the off-season months working as a carpenter at West View Park. As a T.M. Harton Company executive, Beares was responsible for making sure company assets were profitable and successful. Harton awarded his brother in-law with T.M. Harton Company shares on multiple occasions for his dedication to the improvement of the company.

"He took three street cars every day from East Liberty over to West View and was there at 8:00 a.m. to report to work for Ed Vettel, who was T.M.'s gravity engineer."

-Charles Beares III

The park's original Dance Pavilion

A New Revolutionary Roller Coaster Design

At the request of T.M. Harton, Ed Vettel was tasked to design and construct a new unique out and back gravity ride along the park's lake for the following season. In 1910, West View Park unveiled its new signature ride, advertised as The $25,000 Ride. Years later, the ride obtained its most popular name, the Dips. The ride was built on the opposite side of the Mystic Chutes, away from the main midway. To build the ride, management drained the lake and removed a small section to accommodate the loading platform and lift hill. This revolutionary out and back design provided the T.M. Harton Company with further business opportunities to build similar rides elsewhere.

This was the first time the company built a coaster outside the standard Figure Eight and scenic railway design. Compared to the now tame Figure Eight, the ride became an instant favorite with patrons and became known for its many hills and speed. Interestingly enough, when the ride was introduced, it became the first roller coaster in Pennsylvania to feature a hill and drop over fifty feet. In addition, the sensational ride was said to be the longest roller

Lake Placid was drained for the Dips construction

Showcasing the original ride profile of the Dips

coaster ride in Pennsylvania. The ride was modified in 1912 and renamed Leap-the-Dips. By the end of the decade in 1919, the ride received another design modification. T.M. Harton encouraged Ed Vettel to update the ride as technology advanced.

When West View Park's general manager, Oliver MacKalip, passed away in October 1913, J.H. Maxwell, previously of Rock Springs Park, located in Chester, West Virginia, was hired to succeed him. Due to the impact of World War I, Maxwell, with support from ownership, focused on beautifying the park. He added numerous trees and landscaping because the addition of major rides slowed down.

In spite of the war, the park did add attractions to the park. These attractions included a new funhouse dubbed Hilarity Hall in 1915 and the Speed-O-Plane roller coaster in 1917. In 1915, the lease on the park's property ended, and instead of renewing the lease like other amusement parks, T.M. Harton elected to purchase the property. In what was a smart and innovative future planning business decision at the time, Harton's decision to buy the land allowed the

West View Park Company to grow and eventually reduce its debt and build a cash reserve. Purchasing the land established West View Park as the long-term permanent home for the T.M. Harton Company.

The original West View corousel

The most significant attraction added to the park during this period was a new carousel that featured jumping horses in 1914. The carousel replaced the original carousel in the existing building on the main midway and operated until the park closed. The West View Park carousel was a mixed machine. It featured carvings from multiple carousels that T.M. Harton purchased from Gustav Dentzel and D.C. Muller Brothers.

America's involvement in World War I greatly impacted the T.M. Harton Company's business model, as the Company was forced to sell off its European

Original Pony Track with the pedestrian bridge

West View Park ball grounds

assets. Unfortunately, the company was forced to strictly focus their efforts in the United States after the start of World War I, as German occupation spread across Europe. By selling these assets, Harton was able to spend $50,000 at West View Park, building the large Speed-O-Plane roller coaster, replacing the Mystic Chute water ride. The ride was designed using similar roller coaster design techniques and technology used on the Dips roller coaster. While the Park added a new major attraction, West View Park and other amusement parks around the country were forced to impose a war tax on amusements. Prior to the start of the 1917 operating season, the United States declared war in April. As the draft for American troops started, the federal government looked for ways to raise money for the war efforts.

World War I

On June 9, 1917, A.S. McSwigan, representing Kennywood Park, and George Harton, representing West View Park, lobbied against the proposed war tax on amusements in Washington DC to the Senate Committee. The basis of McSwigan's and Harton's disagreement with the bill was the imposing of tax on admission tickets. By the late 1910s, both Kennywood and West View were establishing a group sale business, attracting area school children to have

The streetcar or trolley stop was located by the Pedestrian Bridge, on what is now Center Avenue

picnics at their respective parks. By 1918, the National Outdoor Showmen's Association formed a parks division within its organization to bring park representatives together. By 1920, membership declined and McSwigan saw the opportunity to build an organization that would focus on legislation, insurance, relationship building, safety, and enjoyment of the amusement business. That organization is now known as IAAPA, International Association of Amusement Parks and Attractions. Just as A.S. McSwigan was lobbying for the amusement industry, George Harton was doing the same. Both gentlemen saw the potential of the industry and how it greatly impacted the local economy and the people it serves.

T.M. selected his brother to accompany McSwigan to Washington because of his legal background. It is clear that both individuals went on their own initiative, united with one voice, because management at West View and Kennywood believed amusement parks were pivotal to family entertainment and necessary, especially during the difficult time when families were being separated from loved ones.

World War I impacted the evolution of the amusement park industry. Business models changed, especially due to the outbreak of the 1918 flu pandemic commonly referred to as the Spanish flu. Beginning in 1918, the United

States and the rest of the world experienced the deadliest influenza pandemic to date. It has been estimated that about one-third of the planet's population died due to the outbreak. Many of the military personnel involved in World War I succumbed to the illness and/or spread the virus to other areas of the world. The Spanish flu had multiple waves, and the return of military troops from overseas and lack of social distancing allowed the virus to spread quickly and become more deadly.

As the decade and World War I ended, West View Park had some of its best years. Like Kennywood, West View remained competitive, unlike many of the other trolley parks around the city that closed. Because amusement parks were a new fad and an experience people hadn't had before, business remained strong even though times were difficult.

By establishing a home park, T.M. Harton laid the groundwork for the future of West View Park. The company was well positioned to start new projects at West View Park and abroad. Harton had big plans for the 1920s, which brought in a new era for West View Park and the T.M. Harton Company.

Amusement Arena, West View Park, North Side, Pittsburgh, Pa.

This pre-1917 postcard photo was taken from the lift hill of the dips.

For years, patrons could rent a boat on the lake

This path leading up the hill was commonly used by guests entering the park from the streetcar stop or those wanting to visit the dance pavilion, who may have been on the main midway.

The original Pony Track seen here would later become the home of Talkie Temple

The Parks first band stage was added for the 1907 season

This early photo of the Dance Pavilion was taken from the streetcar/trolley stop

The Speed-o-Plane debuted in 1917, replacing the Mystic Chute

Chapter 5

The Beares Era

The 1918 Spanish flu pandemic continued to impact the world, and as 1919 began, a third wave of flu continued to spread throughout the United States and Europe. In early 1919, Marsh Harton became sick with a mild case of influenza that lasted several weeks. Upon returning home from a business trip to Cincinnati, Ohio, in February, Harton became severely ill. Sadly, on March 1, T.M. Harton passed away at his home at the age of 53 from pneumonia.

While the T.M. Harton Company survived World War I, the end of the war meant surviving another type of battle without its founder and needing to fill a void. At an October 17, 1919, meeting held for the Board of Directors of the West View Park Company, the following was said about T.M. Harton's character and legacy:

> "Mr. Harton, because of his worth and efficiency in the position which he occupied, was held in our high esteem, and because of his sterling qualities, kindness of heart, sense of justice, and unswerving loyalty to his friends, gained and enjoyed not only our respect and love but that of all those whose good fortune it was to know him."

It was evident the company would struggle to move on and replace Marsh Harton. George M. Harton II was named the executor of his brother's will and elected president of the T.M. Harton Company. Being that George was the company's legal representative and his brother's closest advisor, the immediate solution was that he assume the role of president. Once appointed executor and president, George Harton II insisted his brother-in-law, Charles Beares Sr., become more involved in overseeing operations of the overall company and at West View Park. Beares Sr., who had been assisting T.M. Harton with managing the company's day-to-day operations, was

T. M. HARTON DIES IN EAST END HOME

Pneumonia Claims Life of Amusement Company Head.

Theodore M. Harton, president of the T. M. Harton Amusement Company, and principal owner of West View Park, died early yesterday morning in his home, 370 South Negley avenue. His death was due to pneumonia.

Mr. Harton was a widely-known amusement man and manufacturer. As an amusement device manufacturer he was one of the best known in this country. He owned amusement enterprises in Europe and Canada, as well as in this country. For many years he was identified with the park at Conneaut Lake.

Mr. Harton was the son of the late P. M. and Emily Harton. He leaves his widow, Mrs. Laura Wallace Harton; a brother, George M. Harton, and two sisters, Mrs. R. H. Jones and Mrs. T. L. Beares.

appointed T.M. Harton Company's vice president, chief operating officer, president of the West View Park Company, and president of all T.M. Harton Company subsidiaries.

In spite of T.M's death, West View Park continued to attract large crowds through well-attended events at evening dances with big name orchestras. Electing to push forward with T.M. Harton's plans for new attractions at West View Park in 1919, George Harton II and Charles Beares Sr. spent about $100,000 in new attractions and in improving existing rides that summer.

When The Whip was unveiled at West View Park in 1919, it became the first ride installed at the park not manufactured by the T.M. Harton Company. Manufactured by the W.F. Mangels Company at a cost of $50,000, the ride was billed as one of the greatest and most sensational devices ever presented as a park attraction in the country. The Leap-the-Dips roller coaster was also rebuilt and improved.

The company and family were hit again with a major loss when on February 3, 1920, George Harton II passed away from cancer. In less than one year, two key individuals behind one of the most successful companies

Until the end of the 1926, patrons had to walk along the Roller Coaster to other park rides and picnic pavilions

The original Pony Track would eventually be relocated to allow room for the new Talkie Temple and lumber sheds

within the amusement industry were gone. Without founder T.M. Harton, the company's lead salesperson, sales for carousel and roller coasters dropped. Hardship continued for the company when board member and partner Edward C. Berger unexpectedly passed away.

It was no question, the T.M. Harton Company was experiencing a leadership crisis and some questioned if the company could survive. When T.M. Harton passed away, his will stated that his ownership of the company be divided up evenly amongst his wife, Laura, and his siblings: brother George and sisters Olive and Jessie. The reason this occurred was so the family could maintain control of the T.M. Harton Company and West View Park. After the passing of George Harton II, internal matters only became more interesting, as Laura Harton, Marsh Harton's widow, who was rather difficult, was bought out of the T.M. Harton Company. Buying out Laura Harton were Olive Harton Jones and Charles and Jessie Beares.

Olive Harton Jones

After the buyout, Charles and Jessie Beares combined to own the most in the T.M. Harton Company and West View Park Company. Olive Harton Jones became the single largest shareholder in the company, while Carice Harton (George Harton II's widow) retained her existing stock holdings. Following the buyout, the Board of Directors elected Olive Harton Jones the new president of the T.M. Harton Company. During and following the rather quiet 1920 season at West View Park, Charles Beares led the company through the completion of its reorganization as a corporation, which was initiated by George Harton II. The Commonwealth of Pennsylvania officially granted the incorporation on November 11, 1920. The void left by the deaths of T.M. Harton, George Harton II, and Edward Berger were now filled.

The Roaring 20's

The 1920s, known as the Roaring Twenties, were a time of economic prosperity. This era led Americans to witness dramatic social and political changes, which led Americans to move outside of cities and settle in areas that became suburbs. Because parks such as West View and Kennywood were located in suburban areas, the parks thrived as attendance increased throughout the decade. It was also during this time that new styles of dancing and fashion were introduced that challenged the traditional standards. One of the attractions at West View Park that saw the biggest increase in attendance was the dance pavilion. The Grand Army and Marine Band were just a couple of the featured performers. Picnics continued to grow, and many of the local schools continued the tradition of annual picnic days, as did numerous local organizations and churches.

Charles Beares installed an early version of the Tumble Bug, dubbed Joy Plane, in 1923. Interestingly enough, Beares installed a second carousel the same year at West View Park on the top of the hill toward the athletic field. It was not a common practice for parks in the early years to feature two full-sized carousels.

The Joy Plane operated at the park from 1923-1928

The athletic field, which had many uses over the years, became the home venue for a semi-professional football team led by Paul J. Muzzio. Admission to games cost 50 cents, and crowds grew up to 5,000. Between 1919 and 1932, the team entertained crowds and even won the 1927 championship in front of 8,000 fans at West View Park. The popularity of the athletic field and the demand for more grandstand seating gave management the initiative to start work on a new field and expanded grandstand in October 1924 for the following season. Included in the remodel were a running track, baseball diamond, and other features. At a cost of over $25,000, the renovated athletic field became a popular spot for children games and group picnic festivities. Pittsburgh Pirates legend Honus Wagner helped design the new athletic field at West View Park. Until 1933, Pennsylvania Blue Laws prohibited professional sports on Sundays; however, West View Borough was able to work around the laws due to the Muzzio's influence on local politics. Muzzio, a well-known sports promoter during the time period, helped lead the efforts to bring the National Football League to Pittsburgh. The big crowds and popularity of football at West View Park helped the Rooneys secure a professional football franchise in 1933. An accomplished diver, Muzzio was brought in by Beares on special occasions such as Memorial Day, July 4th, and Labor Day to perform a swan

During the 1920s, the ballfield saw an increase in use by park guests

The original administration building, proudly displayed the West View Park Company name above the entry door

dive act off the Dips roller coaster into the lake below.

The park was experiencing growth in popularity, and Beares needed assistance with running day-to-day operations. Shortly after graduating from Princeton University, Charles Beares' son, Charles Jr., began working at West View Park. Known as Nip, Chuck, and Junior by industry friends, Charles Jr. had made a name for himself in his youth through athletics. During his youth and in the summers, Charles Jr. worked as a ride operator on the family's rides at Conneaut Lake Park. He also traveled frequently with his father to the various T.M. Harton Company ride concessions. Charles Jr. attended Peabody High School in Pittsburgh and earned a letter in every sport. He was an all-scholastic quarterback and set numerous school records while being a member of the track team. In addition, he was also a member of the basketball and hockey teams. After graduating from Peabody, Charles Jr. attended Princeton University, where he again starred on the football, basketball, and track and field teams. In 1924, he competed for a spot on the United States Olympic track and field team.

Upgrades continued with the installation of a new drainage system throughout West View Park. Since the inaugural season, the park midways were dirt and stones, unlike the paved midways of parks today. Prior to 1925, inclement weather would

Charles Beares II

Charlie Jr. proudly holding a young pony at the parks pony track

hamper business, as mud would form during rainstorms and water would pool until it dried, as it didn't have anywhere to go. All paths throughout the park had been covered with gravel to avoid guests being inconvenienced during inclement weather. Beares Sr. also built a shelter at the trolley stop, so travelers would not become stuck in the rain while at the park. Advertised as a park with natural beauty, management continued to plant new trees yearly to give the property the wooded appearance founder T.M. Harton had always wanted, keeping areas of the property undeveloped.

In 1925, Charles Beares Sr. sold the Regent Theater in New York and dissolved the Harton Theater Company. That same year, his nephew Howell C. Beares was named the new general manager of West View Park, a position he held through 1930. When asked about the improvements made to the park for the 1925 season, Howell Beares told the *Pittsburgh Press*:

> "With our new improved athletic field, we have booked a record number of good amateur baseball games this year. And changes have been made in the other attractions in anticipation of entertaining the greatest number of guests this year that ever came to West View. Our growth has been steady and consistent, not sensational, but the popularity of the park has increased every year in the same constant manner."

West View Park Expands

The increased business allowed management to construct five new picnic pavilions. These picnic pavilions were built for convenience of group outings and were equipped with hot and cold water and gas ranges. West View Park was in the midst of the first of two major expansions in the park's history. Beares Sr. purchased land outside the park's entrance, as it was deemed necessary to accommodate an estimated 3,000 more automobiles, as more families began to own them. The completion of Perry Highway from all points in Pittsburgh made West View even more accessible to patrons traveling by automobile. With the growing popularity and success of the new Idora Park Jack Rabbit, West View Park needed a new major roller coaster. While the Dips had been lengthened in 1923, management determined West View needed a new major roller coaster much different than the others. Ed Vettel was fascinated with the racing coaster concept in a similar way that Elwood Salsbury once explained: "The racing coaster created a rage for rides."

Charles Sr. was initially hesitant with the idea, but after being convinced by Vettel and son, Charles Jr., planning for the new roller coaster and new main midway began. Vettel knew that, based on industry trends, the main midway needed to be expanded to allow for future ride expansion and revenue-generating opportunities. Prior to the 1927 season, guests had to walk

A train of riders on the Roller Coaster crests the lift hill – 1924

The Racing Whippet debuted in 1927

along a path along the right side of the park's first Figure Eight roller coaster to get to the back of the property. Behind the roller coaster sat the Caterpillar and Joy Plane rides.

In 1927, the Racing Whippet debuted at the far corner of previously undeveloped property and deemed as a replacement to the older Figure Eight roller coaster, which was dismantled. Costing $75,000, the Racing Whippet was the first roller coaster to utilize Ed Vettel's unique shallow track design. The Racing Whippet was unique in that it took advantage of the natural terrain at the back of the property. The loading station for the ride actually straddled a valley in the park. Utilizing the natural topography, the Racing Whippet had a deceiving look, as most of the ride hugged the land. Until the final ride in 1977, the Racing Whippet was one of the Park's most popular rides, second behind the Dips.

Similarly, Kennywood opened a new racing coaster in 1927 as well, simply known as the Racer. Replacing the original Racer, the T.M. Harton Company owned stock in the Kennywood Racing Company, as it was purchased through acquisition of Fred Ingersoll's assets. Both racing coasters were wildly popular, and the Racing Whippet lived up to its name and reputation.

With the Figure Eight roller coaster dismantled, the Beares family focused on landscaping and developing the midway. The original arcade building was torn down and replaced with a newer and larger arcade designed by Ed Vettel. Among the six new buildings, Beares Sr. decided to build two large dining rooms. He also introduced a new free entertainment stage located next to the new administration building. Son Charles Beares Jr. was instrumental in putting together the layout for the building and assisted Ed Vettel with the design of the new administration building that was built on the newly created midway space. Charles Beares III shared what he remembered about the office:

"The two of them (Charles Beares Sr. & Charles Beares Jr.) had offices. My father designed the office at the center of the park. They each had a desk there that faced each other. I remember when I was young, they had all the machines on the first floor that counted all the money. The first aid station was down there."

The parks original Caterpillar was supplied by the Traver Engineering Company

With the additional expense and yearly beautification projects that occurred along with the addition of new trees, flower beds, and general landscaping, management spent over $100,000 improving West View for the 1927 season. As the years went by, Charles Beares Jr. assumed more responsibilities at West View Park while his father traveled frequently to Walbridge Park and Conneaut Lake Park. In July 1927, Charles L. Beares Sr. joined A.W. Robertson, president of the Philadelphia Company, and Homer S. Tripp, vice president and cashier of Merchants National Bank, as newly appointed members to the Board of Directors for the Conneaut Lake Company. Beares was also appointed to the Executive Committee. The changes, which were announced at a Board of Directors meeting held at Hotel Conneaut, reflected a new direction to increase revenue. The following year, in 1928, Beares became president.

Starting in 1928, a new policy was implemented to include free entertainment regularly at Conneaut Lake Park. The concept had been successful at West View Park, and Beares Sr. believed it would prove successful at Conneaut. Another major change focused on orchestra performances, as no single orchestra would play any longer than two weeks. Beares Sr. remained an advisor and member of the Conneaut Lake Park management team until his death in 1954. Interestingly enough, the Beares family maintained a residence for years at Conneaut Lake near the Henningers, former business partners in West View, Conneaut, and now owners of Kennywood. Charles Beares Sr. remained active in the development of Conneaut Lake Park, as he saw the investment as a way to generate additional revenue to improve West View Park.

Because the Racing Whippet created unparalleled excitement for new rides and roller coasters, West View Park invested in a new roller coaster in each of the next two seasons. Charles Beares determined it was necessary to redesign the older Speed-O-Plane roller coaster into an even larger ride called the Greyhound in 1928. The following year, the Dips underwent a dramatic redesign and layout change. It was at this time the famed and fondly remembered Lovers' Tunnel and turnaround (known as the Devil's Bend or Curve) next to Route 19 were added to the ride. The Lovers' Tunnel was a concrete tunnel the Dips train entered as it was dispatched from the loading station. When the operator released the station brakes, the train dipped down and entered a tunnel that circled under the loading station to the bottom of the lift hill.

During the 1927 offseason, the Speed-o-Plane was redesigned, enlarged, and given a new name. The Greyhound debuted in 1928 and operated through the 1945 summer

The tunnel became the location of many Pittsburghers' first kiss. As a kid, Andy Vettel (Ed's nephew) created the drawing for the now famous bend, while his uncle engineered the actual design. Costing $32,000 to convert the ride from a side-friction coaster, the Dips went on to become the most popular ride at the park. Advertised as one the highest and fastest gravity rides in the United States, the ride met with much success, and management was proud to unveil what they believed to be the most exciting roller coaster experience in the country. The ride's famous turnaround next to Route 19 became a symbol for the park. Onlookers would wait by the turn, waiting for the train to come screeching by as riders held on for their safety and the train maneuvered through the tight, banked curve. The ride was known to be thrilling and death-defying. Over the years, some deaths did occur on the ride, mainly because riders disregarded safety warnings of not standing up and unbuckling their seat belt.

Along with the new Dips, Charles Beares Sr. installed a new Tumble Bug by the Racing Whippet, replacing the Joy Plane. The ride was purchased from the Traver Engineering Company, who previously sold the park the Caterpillar. Roughly $18,000 was spent on new landscaping, flower beds, trees, and picnic facilities. Located in nearby Beaver Falls, owner Harry Traver was an industry businessman famous for selling multiple rides such as the Circle Swing, Caterpillar, and Tumble Bug. He was a noted salesman of early dark rides and a new twister style wooden roller coaster with steel structures.

As with the rest of the 1920s, 1929 was another successful year for West View. The dance pavilion was hosting crowds of unusual size and broke the previous season attendance records. West View Park was experiencing great prosperity and expansion. For the 1930 season, Beares Sr. purchased a Cuddle Up from Berk Engineering. The West View Park Company paid a third down with the order and two-thirds upon receipt of the ride. The purchase was practically a cash transaction.

Ed Vettel's shallow track design featured track ties near the top layer of wood in the track. Vettel believed his design kept the track in gauge better than other designs, allowing for less vibration, superstructure and a smoother ride for his articulating trains.

"In answer to your letter of the 10th in regard to our Cuddle Up, we are very well satisfied with the revenue that we derived from it. We took in over $7,000.00 and had no mechanical trouble at all…. Everyone seemed to like this ride, as we always had a lineup waiting their turn. We would consider this a great amusement for any park."

- C.L. Beares Sr. President, West View Park Company

The T.M. Harton Company was broken up into multiple holding companies. Over the years, West View Park Company operated rides in the park as separate businesses, similar to how other parks operated. In most cases, these companies were established when a new ride was purchased. Examples of this model were the Racing Whippet Company and West View Whip Company. The West View Refreshment Company was also one of the subsidiary companies held within West View Park Company. Throughout the decade, many of the roller coasters, carousel, and other ride concessions were sold off to the owners of the respective parks; the T.M. Harton Company elected to retain its most profitable concessions at other parks, such as Conneaut Lake Park, Cedar Point, and Walbridge Park. Starting in 1923, Beares Sr. began selling off many of the concessions in Europe. Domestically, the company retained the most profitable concession, which included Cedar Point in Sandusky, Ohio, because Harry Covode was stationed at nearby Walbridge Park in Toledo.

In light of the growing popularity of roller coasters, Ed Vettel took the opportunity to consult with and design new roller coasters for other parks. Vettel worked out of an office adjacent to the maintenance shop located down the hill behind the dance hall. Featured on the walls of the office were various designs for rides. With the success of the West View roller coaster designs, Willow Grove Park, located just outside of Philadelphia, opened the Ed Vettel-designed Thunderbolt roller coaster in 1931 for the Dayton Fun House & Manufacturing Company (later known as National Amusement Device). The ride operated until the park closed in 1975.

The Willow Grove Thunderbolt

The Depression Years

Known as Black Thursday, the October 24, 1929, stock market crash remains the worst in United States history. The Great Depression impacted income, employment opportunities, and the economy. The country's industrial and agricultural businesses were hit especially hard by the severe economic down-turn. The Great Depression made it difficult for all businesses to stay afloat, not just amusement parks. While West View's rides suffered to bring in the large amount of revenue brought in during the 1920s, the ballroom brought in the most revenue during the 1930s. Dancing and social gatherings allowed the park to survive the Great Depression. Roller skating was introduced in 1933 and continued throughout the fall and winter season to allow for year-round revenue. The dance pavilion was closed in during the fall and winter months and heated, utilizing potbelly stoves. During the winter months, guests could also ice skate on the lake.

In 1931, Frank L. Danahey, who previously worked at Kennywood, was named general manager of West View Park to replace Howell C. Beares. Danahey had held a senior management role at Kennywood before accepting his new job at West View Park. Known in the industry as a picnic expert, Danahey was a quintessential salesman. He believed in keeping a strong line of communication with each picnic client in order to retain business the following year. At the time, West View Park's group business was not as strong as Kennywood's. Picnic pavilions and groves were frequently used, but it was Danahey who established higher standards for the park's group sales business. Within two years, West View Park hosted larger sized picnics and events, including the Newspapermen of Pittsburgh and the local Seckatary Hawkins Club, and established a Farm and Flower Show. Under Frank L. Danahey's direction, West View Park even added a 100 by 200-foot swimming pool with a sand beach, which opened in 1932 at the bottom of the depression.

Upon graduating from Princeton University in 1926, Charles Beares Jr. began taking an active role in managing the park. He actively managed park operations during this time and was groomed to be the eventual general manager of West View Park. He had grown up in the amusement industry, traveling with his parents often, seeing both Conneaut Lake Park and West View Park grow and prosper. In 1933, he was named general manager of the West View Park, replacing Frank Danahey. Danahey returned to Kennywood and remained a key part of the management team until the late 1950s. As his father did before him, Charles Beares Jr. quickly became acquainted with other owners and managers in the industry. He became good friends with the members of the newly formed Pennsylvania Amusement Park Association (PAPA). From its formation in 1935, Beares held the position of PAPA treasurer until 1948, when changes occurred to allow for a rotation of Pennsylvania park leaders to hold positions on the organization's board of directors. In addition, he held board positions within the NAAPPB (National Association of Amusement Parks, Pools, & Beaches) and quickly earned the reputation of being a savvy amusement park manager.

In 1932, West View hosted the Fearless Falcons, a high pole act as a part of the free entertainment shows held every summer. It was during this 1932 show when Charles Beares Jr. met Inez Hubbell. Performing one hundred feet in the air on a sway pole, Inez had previously performed with her three sisters as a member of the Flying Wards, a well-known family of trapeze artists. Eventually, she joined her sisters in Sels Floto, considered the second most popular circus in the country, only behind Ringling Brothers and Barnum & Bailey Circus. She later joined her brother-in-law, Tom Mix, with the Tom Mix Circus. Beares and Hubbell married in 1936 and had a son, Charles Beares III, the first third generation member of the Harton family.

Never having lost his interest in the local sports scene, Beares Jr. was impressed with the play of Carnegie Tech (now Carnegie Mellon University) fullback Johnny Karcis and offered him a job as a police officer at West View Park. After graduation, Karcis went on to play football professionally for the Brooklyn Dodgers, Pittsburgh Steelers, Boston Redskins, and New York Giants. Karcis was a member of the New York Giants when they won the NFL title in 1938.

By the mid-1930s, both West View Park and Kennywood had strong business models and some of the best management found in the amusement industry. The strong financial backing of the Harton family held West View competitive with Kennywood. By 1936, West View Park was controlled by family stockholders Jessie Beares, Olive Harton Jones, and Carice Patterson (George Harton II's widow). These family members owned 75 percent with Charles Sr., Jessie's husband, who owned an additional 20 percent. Other relatives and employees owned the remaining 5 percent.

During the Depression, most parks were hesitant to declare business satisfactory. Discouraging labor and unemployment conditions impacted most parks and businesses. Parks lost money during that time, and West View was one of them. While most ride and attractions lost money, the roller coasters and dance pavilion remained profitable and carried the park.

The father and son management duo recognized that the dance pavilion was driving revenue, and so they decided to install a new maple floor in 1935. With the help of radio, big band music was also becoming increasingly popular. Local radio stations KDKA and KQV held multiple live summer broadcasts from the West View Park ballroom throughout the 1930s and 1940s. Big name bands and orchestras such as Tommy Tucker, Jack Peck, Lee Crosley, Danny Nirella, Baron Elliott, and Benny Burton provided the dance music for the large weekly dances. The location of the ballroom at West View Park also proved to be crucial to the park's success. Since the streetcar or trolley stop was located next to the entrance of the ballroom, the few hundred feet walk allowed patrons to have an easy walk to the venue. West View Park survived the Depression and emerged with strength in the 1930s.

Park announcer Russell Linhart's booming voice could be heard on park midways from 1933 to 1942 until World War II interrupted his park career. Serving three years in the military, he returned to the park in 1945 and stayed on through 1952. Linhart, who originally sold balloons on the midway, obtained the announcer position and learned how to operate the public address system over a two-day period. While it was common for no formal training to occur, Linhart eventually took up the responsibility of being emcee for acts at the dance pavilion. The radio tower located on the midway across from the arcade housed the public address system.

Changes at Conneaut Lake Park & Walbridge Park

Since the Great Depression hurt business, many parks decided not to invest in new attractions for fear of not being able to sustain operations. In spite of the Great Depression, Ed Vettel stayed busy designing and building a children's roller coaster known as the Kiddie Coaster in 1937 at Idora Park as well as a new gravity ride for Conneaut Lake Park. With Charles Beares Sr. managing the company's interests at Conneaut as well as being an active member of the Conneaut Lake Park management team, it was a relatively easy process to have the T.M. Harton Company design Conneaut Lake Park's new signature ride. Opening on July 4, 1937, the Conneaut Lake Park Blue Streak quickly became the Park's most popular ride. The Blue Streak marked an end of an era for the T.M. Harton Company, as it was the last roller coaster financed, designed, and built by the company.

The T.M. Harton Company had previously owned and managed the Scenic Railway at Conneaut Lake Park. The ride had opened in 1909 and sat on the site now occupied by the Blue Streak roller coaster. Prior to 1910, the T.M. Harton Company purchased the Conneaut Lake Park's other roller coaster, the Jack Rabbit, from Ingersoll Engineering. Ingersoll Engineering had built

The Scenic Railway at Conneaut Lake Park

this ride in 1904. Both the Scenic Railway and the Jack Rabbit were removed after the 1936 season to make way for the new and improved Blue Streak roller coaster. Amusement industry veteran and former Conneaut Lake Park employee Sam Shurgott said:

"The Blue Streak is a shallow track coaster. The weight of the train, in this case, doesn't have a huge bearing on the structure. The Vettel built trains are lighter, but are also shorter. They were very maneuverable, like the GCI (Great Coasters International) Millennium Flyers."

Sam went on to explain all roller coaster designers have their own track design and trains. Ed Vettel used a different track he developed much like that of John Miller, Herbert Schmeck, and John Allen. Vettel used an angle iron rail as an upstop on both Conneaut Lake Park's Blue Streak and West View Park's Dips. According to Shurgott, West View's Racing Whippet used a standard track design, as he (Ed Vettel) was probably still perfecting his own track design.

John Allen of the Philadelphia Toboggan Company was contracted in the 1960s to reprofile the Blue Streak in the mid-1960s. Shurgott recalled:

"He raised the curve next to Rt 618 16ft, which checked the speed of the newer, heavier NAD (National Amusement Device) trains. The greatest stress on the trains is after that curve, when it hits the twisting transition. The first three hills were that steep when the Vettels built that ride. Allen was also the one who angled the track after the first drop in order to prevent rider injuries. The Blue Streak still has the same system from 1937 that starts the lift motor. It has a 4-speed variable control."

On October 26, 1938, Charles Beares Sr. and Jr. learned Walbridge Park was hit with a catastrophic fire. Unfortunately, the blaze destroyed most of the park attractions, including the 1929 Speedway roller coaster designed by Ed Vettel. Other attractions lost in the blaze were the dance hall, Whip, Skooter, Pretzel (dark ride), Old Mill, and food and game stands. The lone survivor of the fire was the Park's carousel. Even though the T.M. Harton Company was prepared for such a devasting event by having fire insurance, it was estimated to cost around $150,000 to rebuild, leaving Harry Covode and Beares Sr. debating if the park should be rebuilt.

Although fire threatened the future of Walbridge Park, Beares Sr. and Covode vowed to rebuild the park in time for the next summer season; however, the city of Toledo was not in favor of the park being rebuilt. It was then decided under an agreement with city manager John Edy that the park could be rebuilt without the roller coaster and that the carousel organ had to be muted during performances at the Toledo Zoo amphitheater. While the local government wasn't pleased, the amusement center would resurface. The T.M. Harton Company worked quickly to bring in new rides, including a Whip, Pretzel (dark ride), Loop-o-Plane, Skooter bumper cars, and, in 1940, a new Tumble Bug.

Re-inventing of West View Park Picnics

West View Park maintained its popularity throughout the late 1930s. The dance hall continued to host and bring back the country's most popular orchestras. In 1938, the park added its first dark ride, dubbed Ride-N-Laff, next to the Cuddle-Up, along the midway near the Dips. The attraction was man-ufactured by the R.E. Chambers Company (the successor company of Traver Engineering). A new Whip with a pavilion and Sportland games building were added to the park and ready for opening day on May 8, 1938.

It was a difficult operating season for the park in 1938. Although the park hosted 138 picnics compared to 134 the previous season, income was down roughly 25 percent. To produce income while hiring very little additional staff, the park opened the dance hall for roller skating. On October 29, 1938, General Manager Charles Beares Jr. announced the addition of John P. Hickey to the West View Park staff as picnic booking manager. Hickey was no stranger to the Pittsburgh amusement scene.

> "John P. Hickey, for the past five years with Idlewild Park, Ligonier, Pa., and Rock Springs Park, Chester, West Virginia., and before that Olympia Park, McKeesport, Pa., has joined the staff of West View Park here, it was announced by Park Manager Charles L. Beares Jr."
>
> *-The Billboard, November 5, 1938*

Even with the dip in revenue, school picnics remained the lifeblood of the business.

> "Each Catholic grade school in the area had a picnic day just for them ... mine was Nativity G.S. Day. We lived for this day because we could jump on the 10 West View street car ... not trolley ... and within 10 minutes be in the park, most of the time alone. Our parents would come later and convene in the bar on site. But the key to the day was that each bunch of friends dressed alike, boys and girls. The worst was the year we boys, about six of us, decided to wear snap brim hats. Most were knocked off our heads in the first hour. The girls had matching poodle skirts or capri pants or bouffant hairstyles with matching headbands. Awful sights. I lived on or near Perrysville Avenue most of my youth. The "Avenue" was the direct route to the park, serviced by the 10 West View and the 8 Perrysville (streetcar)."
>
> *Bob Mill – Sewickley, PA*

A machinist by trade, Hickey was looking for a new career when he applied and was hired for the position of book manager at Olympia Park, located just outside his hometown of McKeesport, Pennsylvania. Olympia Park was part of the Olympia-Oakford Park Company, a management company led by Henry E. Hampe. School picnics that originated at Olympia and Oakford Park under John Hickey continue to this day at Kennywood. While Olympia Park did not feature any T.M. Harton attractions, Oakford Park featured a T.M. Harton Figure Eight, carousel, and carousel building. The Oakford Park carousel building was similar in design to the carousel building that can still be found at Idlewild & SoakZone in Ligonier. Upon seeing the opportunity to grow the picnic

John P. Hickey

business at West View Park, Hickey joined the management team and helped attract more than 200 picnics and groups to the park in one season.

"One of the major highlights of the school year was the school picnic that occurred at the end of every school year at West View Park. I recall early morning, the day of the school picnic, my father bringing our large picnic basket to our church. I recall all of us school children singing songs to the bus driver during our trip to West View Park. We would all meet in a pavilion to enjoy the food my mother prepared for dinner. I remember all the fun we had playing the games and riding the rides. We would spend the entire day at West View Park until dark. We took 2 streetcars home from the park because not many families had cars then. I recall that after I got much older, married, and had children, a very good friend of ours was employed with Mellon Bank. Mellon Bank's yearly employee picnic was held at West View Park. Our friend would invite us to go to the bank's picnic and it was great to share my memories with our children."

Theresa Prodente Balzer - Penn Hills, PA

In 1939, the Pennsylvania Amusement Park Association (PAPA), later renamed Pennsylvania Amusement Parks and Attractions, held its annual summer meeting at West View Park. At the time, President E.E. Foehl of

Kauffmann's Department Store Picnic

Willow Grove Park, located outside Philadelphia, headed the organization. Willow Grove Park was home to the popular Vettel-designed Thunderbolt roller coaster, with its swooping drops and curves. The annual summer PAPA meeting returned to West View Park again in 1945. In a 1945 letter, PAPA President T.C. Foley said:

> "Our host, Charles Beares, Jr., assisted by Brady McSwigan, has informed me that they have arranged some special features for this meeting. You all know that when these boys set out to do a job, they do it in a big way."

The Development of Vettel Roller Coasters

An interesting story of the late 1930s came about when Ben Krashner, owner of Lakeside Amusement Park near Denver, Colorado, began visiting parks. During these visits, Krashner became impressed with the Zephyr roller coaster in operation at Pontchartrain Beach Amusement Park in New Orleans. Opening in 1939, the Pontchartrain Beach Amusement Park Zephyr operated until the park closed after the 1983 season. An out and back roller coaster,

The Zephyr

originally the Zephyr featured a low to the ground turnaround similar to the one found on the Conneaut Lake Blue Streak. The Zephyr turnaround was redesigned and reflected a similar design as the banked turnaround on the Dips at West View Park. The Zephyr became a symbol of the park, and patrons became familiar with the tower located at the top of its lift hill. The Batt family, owners of Pontchartrain Beach Amusement Park, were pleased with the ride Ed Vettel Sr. designed. The Zephyr remained one of the most popular rides in the park's history.

In an October 3, 1947, letter to Brady McSwigan, president of Kennywood Park, Harry Batt Sr. wrote:

> "We suffered about $2500.00 worth of water damage to merchandise, and the other damage was very light; I don't believe that it totaled over $4000.00 tops. All of the high rides were undamaged and not a stick of lumber was blown off our coaster, which speaks well for the Vettel construction."

Designed for NAD (National Amusement Device Company), the ride was one of the longest roller coasters Vettel Sr. ever designed. The ride was built with the help of T.M. Harton employees, most notably Ed Vettel Jr. and West View Park carpenter Ivan Murray. With the success of the Zephyr, Ben Krashner contacted Ed Vettel Sr. and asked him to design a new roller coaster for Lakeside Amusement Park. The end result was the Cyclone roller coaster, which opened on May 17, 1940. In a Sunday, March 31, 1940, *Pittsburgh Press* news article, Ed Vettel Sr., said:

Ed Vettel Jr. and Ivan Murray

> "Years ago, it was considered daring to build a dip four to ten feet high. Many park owners thought the drop was too steep. Today on our Denver ride, the first drop is more than 90 feet. In all, the ride covers 4300 feet of track, the largest we have tackled."

The ride features an Art Deco designed loading station with neon lights, a light-up safety board, Ed Vettel designed trains, and a tunnel at the beginning of the ride. When asked in 1940 about the youth and the progression of roller coasters, Ed Vettel Sr. explained:

The Cyclone

> "No Sir, I don't know what we'll do with the younger generation. You can't give them gravity rides daring enough. There doesn't seem to be dips deep enough nor curves sharp enough for them."

The Lakeside Amusement Park Cyclone

Entertainment at West View Park

On April 27, 1940, Charles L. Beares Jr. announced the park would open for its thirty-fifth season on May 12. West View Park was still very much an entertainment destination and had been hosting opening acts to kick off each season for many years. Local and name orchestras for dancing were booked in the new redecorated dance hall starting on May 23 with Fran Eichler. The most noticeable change occurring that year was the creation of a new parking area in what was once part of the park's lake. A new auto entrance was added to the north end of the property, allowing access from Route 19 for the first time. The new parking lot would be able to accommodate up to 500 automobiles. This was the first time the lake was partially filled in to accommodate the change in needs by Pittsburghers.

Entertainment remained a huge draw for the park, as another entertainment venue opened in 1941. The new Talkie Temple outdoor amphitheater, with its modernistic shell design and large seating area, was constructed on the site of the original Talkie Temple outdoor stage, which had opened on the same site in 1933. This had been the original site of the pony track, before it was relocated to the top of the hill by the athletic field.

The Talkie Temple hosted many acts throughout the years. These performances included magic acts, variety shows, wrestling matches, bands, and so much more. Known as talkie shows, or simply talkies, evening entertainment was a common crowd pleaser at the park, especially on Sundays. During the Depression, the park continued to host talkies every Sunday night, weather permitting, after Labor Day.

The word *temple* was commonly used at the time to describe a band shell and the word *talkie* was used to describe up and coming or current popular acts performing on what used to be vaudeville stages. The word also has its origin from motion picture theaters, in which the company was invested; in other words, moving pictures with sound or talking pictures. According to the Harton family, the new outdoor entertainment venue was named by Charles Beares Jr. Talkie Temple was modeled after the popular Hollywood Bowl band shell. Known for its arches and setting in California, Talkie Temple was West View's attempt to bring outdoor entertainment of all varieties to the crowds of Pittsburgh.

The War Years

Introduced in 1941, and brought back in 1943, the park held a ten-day fireworks show over the lake called the Festival of Fire. This popular event was met with pleasing results and continued for future seasons. Post WWII, the Park would disrupt the night sky by ending each day with Fireworks from July 4th to Labor Day. For those who lived in the community, it provided entertainment and excitement for anyone who may not have had the funds to visit the park.

For most of WWII, the park invested little into new rides, although a Mangel's kiddie Ferris wheel and pony cart ride opened in 1942, with the first incarnation of Kiddieland. Ongoing afternoon and evening stage shows occurred daily throughout the season. On Sundays, holidays, and for some particular organizations, concerts or staged shows were held at Talkie Temple, which had an audience capacity of approximately 4,000. The Talkie Temple and free act stage would help open the park on opening day with free entertainment. Amateur boxing matches and various contests became a common draw for guests. Picnics and outings at the park were growing, and while the rides provided entertainment, so did the games for children at the park's athletic field.

The dance business, not just at West View, was a significant moneymaker, especially during the war years. In 1944, Charles Beares Jr. hired Jack Stoll as the new dance pavilion manager, replacing Bill Bodan. Beares' idea of using the dance pavilion as a roller skating rink provided the much needed revenue to sustain a profit. During WWII, the park held patriotic events with fireworks displays. On Memorial Day and the Fourth of July, the park became crowded with guests.

During the 1940s, in addition to his duties at West View Park, Charles Jr. accepted and held a Board of Directors position with the NAAPPB. Years later, this organization changed its name to the IAAPA. The war rations on materials made owning and operating a business difficult. People traveled little during this era and spent less money.

Management was optimistic the war would end soon and economic conditions would change for the better. Many parks struggled to maintain proper staffing levels. Women began working more during the war and began taking on jobs previously held by men. While the installation of new attractions was limited, the park did add new games and food buildings in the 1940s.

Picnic Manager John P. Hickey and General Manager Charles L. Beares Jr. were instrumental in hosting the big Junior Commando picnic at West View Park on July 28, 1943. Races, games, rides, entertainment, and prizes were all organized with the help of Commando-in-Chief Frank E. Murray and the *Pittsburgh Post-Gazette* newspaper. Twelve thousand Junior Commandos found their way to the park for the picnic event.

West View Park management provided the *Pittsburgh Post-Gazette* with strips of tickets, consisting of ten tickets per strip. Each ticket was good for admission to any of the park attractions. Junior Commandos was the name used for youth organizations to show support for the war effort. The Junior Commandos were inspired by a children's comic book. They salvaged scrap metal that could be recycled for the war effort.

The park continued to schedule and host numerous picnics during the summer season. Picnics in the early 1940s included Gimbels department stores, Duquesne Heights Civic Association, Bethlehem Steel Company, Owen-Illinois Can Company, and Pittsburgh Forgings Company.

John Hickey (left) and Chief Frank Murray (right) watch as General Manager Charles Beares Jr signs the contract for the 1943 Junior Commando picnic

"Every spring, West View Park would have special school picnic days. Our family would always go on Assumption Days. We would get strips of tickets for the rides at the school, my mom would pack a lunch, and the family would take the trolley to the park. We spent the whole day riding as many amusement rides as possible, and we would always enjoy sticky pink cotton candy on a stick. The amazing thing was Mom and Dad would put our picnic basket full of food on a table in the pavilion. It would sit untouched by others until we were ready to eat. Automobiles were scarce, and visitors rode trolleys from downtown to the park's entrance for a nickel. The Dips and Racing Whippet coasters were the park's most heavily patronized rides, but dancing and roller skating in the West View ballroom were also popular."

Chuck Brunner – Dedham, MA

Boasting over forty rides and attractions, such as games, food stands, and entertainment venues, the park's sixty-eight acres of oak-shaded woodland was also the home to seven spacious dining pavilions and numerous tables in the picnic groves. Ten of these acres were devoted to five parking lots. The park continued to progress forward as the mid-1940s arrived. After each season, the park continued to see an increase in attendance and revenue. J.R. Henry, who worked at West View from 1971 to 1976, recalled, every picnic pavilion was numbered:

> "There were seven large pavilions. The large #5 pavilion was located by Boot Hill, #s 6 and 7 were the double-decker pavilion in Kiddieland, #4 Pavilion overlooked the midway, #3 was by the bridge, and behind #5 was a strip of land for picnic tables. This was the property located behind the administration building."

The company started 1946 on a somber note, as Harry Covode, general manager of Walbridge Park, unexpectedly passed away. Appointed as acting general manager was West View Park General Manager Charles Beares Jr., who would only hold the position temporarily. Little did Charles Beares Sr. and Jr. know that the end of WWII would mark an unexpected change in leadership for the T.M. Harton Company and West View Park.

Shortly before her death in December 1945, Olive Harton Jones was convinced to alter two trusts holding her T.M. Harton Company stock by the company's secretary treasurer, Charles Cain. Charles Beares Jr. was the original and lone heir in one trust, with the third generation of Hartons (Charles Beares III, Janet Harton, and George Harton IV) named beneficiaries in the other. The two rather complicated trusts were rewritten to make Janet and George IV beneficiaries in both trusts and Charles Beares III remaining as a beneficiary in one of the two trusts. Olive Harton Jones was persuaded by Cain that her sister and brother-in-law would make their son (Charles Jr.) and grandson (Charles III) beneficiaries of their stock following their deaths and removed him as an heir in her trusts. The Beareses were unprepared when at the March 1946 stockholders' meeting, Carice (Harton) Kountz was able to vote out of power both Charles Beares Sr. and Charles Beares Jr.

Feeling conflicting thoughts about the situation, Charles Cain attempted to vote the Beares family back into power, a decision that led to his dismissal from the company. Upset by decisions made at the stockholders' meeting, Charles Sr. and Jessie Beares elected to sell their holdings in the T.M. Harton Company in the fall of 1948 to Carice Kountz. Carice Patterson, who remarried to A. Edward Kountz following the death of her third husband, now owned 60 percent of the Company, making her the new majority owner and largest single stockholder in the T.M. Harton Company and West View Park Company. The rewritten trusts set up by Olive Harton Jones were now deemed meaningless, and the balancing of power between both sides of the family, as Olive Harton Jones wanted, did not occur. With the Beares family voted out of power, Carice Kountz voted her shares to elect her son George Harton III as president of the T.M. Harton Company and general manager of West View Park.

Jessie, Charles III, and Charles Beares, Sr.

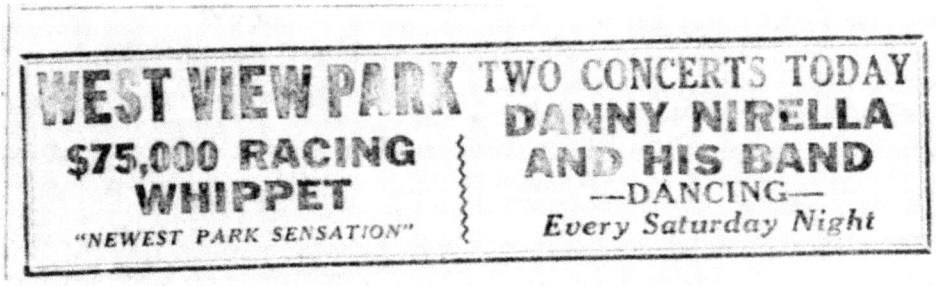

The Talkie Temple became the new home for entertainment

THE PITTSBURGH PRESS
TUESDAY, DECEMBER 1, 1936

PARK MEN ATTEND CHICAGO CONVENTION

Preview of Amusements Will Feature Sessions

A preview of what the amusement park patrons will enjoy next summer will be shown Pittsburghers attending the eighteenth annual convention of the National Association of Amusement Parks, Pools and Beaches in Chicago today. Among the new things the park men will see are swing style bathing suits, cellophane-wrapped merry-go-round rings and streamlined frankfurters.

Five hundred persons are attending from all parts of the country. The Western Pennsylvania delegation is one of the largest groups. It includes managers and officials from two parks. They are Kennywood— Andrey Brady McSwigan, president; Frederick W. Henninger, vice president and secretary; A. J. Wyant, manager; John F. McTighe, Robert W. Comstock and Carl E. Henninger. West View—C. L. Beares, president; Walter Williams, secretary and treasurer, and C. L. Beares Jr., manager.

When prohibition ended, West View began selling beer in 1934 and also permitted beer at its picnics. Kennywood elected to remain a dry park

The new administration building was designed by Ed Vettel Sr., and Charles Beares Jr.

The T.M. Harton Company Idlewild Carousel Pavilion as seen in the 1930s

The strong financial backing of
the T.M. Harton Company, Olive
Harton Jones, and Jessie and
Charles Beares, helped West View
Park survive the Depression.

In 1937, a new dance floor was installed in the dance pavilion, 109 picnics booked for June, and a new fountain with lights was added in the middle of the lake

Families flocked to West View Park for a day of family fun

The Cedar Point High Frolics was designed by Ed Vettel. The ride operated from 1934-1940

The Beares Family took great pride in maintaining their interests at Conneaut Lake Park including the Blue Streak roller coaster. Every September, Charles Beares Sr and Jr would have Ivan Murray and the Vettel's travel to Conneaut for two weeks to work on the Blue Streak.

Management continued to the original vision for the park of maintaining the property's natural beauty with trees, flowers, and overall appearance.

Chapter 6

The George Harton Years

Beares - Harton Transition

A new era for West View Park began in March 1946, as George Harton III was elected president of the T.M. Harton Company. Harton replaced his Aunt Olive, who had been president of the company until her death in December 1945. Recently discharged from the Navy, George Maurice Harton III returned home to run the company that his father and uncle had started in 1893. A lieutenant while in the Navy, Harton attended Shadyside Academy and graduated from Culver Military Academy. Nicknamed Flash Harton, George III was a member of the varsity track team, football, basketball, and baseball teams, and was captain of the football team. A member of the drama club, he was also an ROTC winner of medals in musketry and pistol marksmanship. John Patterson, Harton's stepfather, a prominent Pittsburgher and industrialist involved in the steel and banking industries, groomed his stepson for leadership. At a young age, Patterson showed Harton the importance of hands-on training and learning each position within a business. For a brief period of time, Harton worked in the steel industry; however, he did not favor the industry like his stepfather.

These combined experiences provided leadership training for Harton's life after school and during his years in active military duty. Obtaining a psychology degree in 1936 from Princeton University, George III obtained his law degree from the University of Michigan in 1940 and passed the bar exam, just as his father had done.

During WWII, Harton served in a leadership role as a radar night fighter direction officer aboard the aircraft carrier U.S.S Ticonderoga, which was in Tokyo Bay at the time of the Japanese surrender. Before taking on the role of radar night fighter direction officer, George III was a night fighter who flew and landed planes in the middle of the night.

Interestingly enough, across town at Kennywood, a similar situation occurred. Carl Henninger resumed his duties as vice president and general manager upon returning home after serving almost four years with the United States Navy.

For the transition to be complete, George Harton was appointed West View Park Company president and general manager, replacing his uncle, Charles Beares Sr., and cousin Charles Beares Jr., who became the refreshment manager. Beares Sr. moved to Conneaut Lake and became an advisor to the management team of Conneaut Lake Park, where the T.M. Harton Company owned and operated a carousel, roller coaster, and bingo hall. During the transition period, Charles Sr. and his wife, Jessie, became sole owners of the Conneaut Lake Park amusement operations.

In 1948, Harry Habel joined the West View Park management team and replacing Charles Beares Jr. as the refreshment manager. Like his father, Beares Jr. moved to Conneaut Lake and accepted a management position at the park, after receiving an offer from the park's president and friend, Elmer Freeland. Beares took an active role in the overall management of Conneaut Lake Park and Hotel Conneaut as well as operations of the carousel and Blue Streak. Beares Jr. left Conneaut after the 1950 season to help the Plarr family

George M. Harton III

George M. Harton III, Ed Vettel Jr., and Charles Beares II in Chicago at the industry convention

manage Dorney Park in Allentown, Pennsylvania, before retiring from the business and returning to Conneaut after his parents passed away in late 1953 (Jessie) and 1954 (Charles Sr). When the Beares family permanently relocated to Conneaut Lake, Charles Beares III began working at the park as a ride operator on the family-owned carousel and Blue Streak, working alongside his father. Not long after he retired, Beares Jr. became sick and battled cancer until he succumbed to the disease in 1958. Shortly after the passing of his father in 1954, Charles Beares II sold ownership in the carousel and Blue Streak roller coaster to the ownership team of Conneaut Lake Park. Charlie Beares III explained he worked at both West View Park and Conneaut Lake:

> "I worked at West View informally, as I was 10. I worked at the popcorn stand two or three years. Julia Saam was the popcorn stand manager; she worked at West View from 1920–1947. I worked at Conneaut from the time I was 16 to about 1960. I was the master of ceremonies at Fascination."

While Charles Beares III continued to work at Conneaut Lake Park as a seasonal employee through college, the T.M. Harton Company no longer owned assets outside of West View Park. Conneaut Lake Park was known as a destination for park owners and managers. It was a common location for industry meetings and vacations. George III took regular summer trips to Conneaut Lake Park and took his children so they could en-

joy the park and visit with their cousin. A few weeks were spent each summer at Conneaut Lake Park. While he enjoyed working at the park, Charlie III also enjoyed the lake for recreational purposes, such as water skiing. Once Harton assumed the role of president of the T.M. Harton Company, he went to work introducing himself to prominent figures within the amusement park industry when the opportunity presented itself.

> "Dear Mr. Harton: Just a little note to extend very best wishes in your new capacity as President of T.M. Harton Company. It is the wish of all of us at Kennywood that you will have every success. If at any time we can be of assistance, please feel free to call upon us."
>
> *- A. Brady McSwigan, President, Kennywood Park, NAAPPB*

In an April 26, 1946, letter to Brady McSwigan, president of nearby Kennywood Park and president of NAAPPB, Harton wrote:

> "I certainly will make it a point to find time to take an active part in the amusement park industry, becoming interested in the work of the NAAPPB. I certainly will need help in becoming better acquainted in your organization and wish to thank you for offering to help me do so."

Charles Beares Jr. remained active in the NAAPPB's annual convention. Cousin George joined him in leading seminars and discussing topics with park

Ed Vettel Sr. loved models and designed roller coasters by building models. Ed Jr.,
is seen holding a model of an early design of Idora Park's Kiddie Coaster, while Ed Sr. is
seen next to his latest ride design.

Originally the Racing Whippet was built within the woods, however over the years,
trees were removed for maintenance and safety purposes.

Automobiles arriving to West View Park by Route 19 were greeted by
this sign and column in 1952.

owners and managers. Beares led a session on outstanding promotions and
Harton presented a session on offseason activities. West View Park leadership
was now set for the next twenty years.

Immediately after the 1945 season concluded on Labor Day, Ed Vettel
and his crew began demolition and construction work on West View's second major expansion in its history. Prior to the end of the 1945 season, it
was decided the popular Greyhound roller coaster would be dismantled to
accommodate additional rides and midway space for growing attendance and
future expansion. Charles Beares Jr. worked closely with Ed Vettel designing
the look for the new park midway and games mall. In working with Charles
Jr, and discussing logistics, Vettel designed the new game mall to have storage
space, which was needed to accommodate the growing need for additional
games and prizes. This new layout allowed Games Manager Howard Howell,
better known as Ky, to run a more efficient games operations.

As Vettel finalized all the engineering work and blueprints, Charles Jr.
signed a contract for a new flying scooter ride, Ferris wheel, and miniature
railroad ride. Charles Sr. and Charles Jr. were committed to spending more

than $125,000 for what was to be the most successful year in West View Park's history.

In addition to new rides, new buildings were constructed and older buildings refurbished. Newly installed multicolored neon, fluorescent, and indirect lighting enhanced the new colors that donned the midway. While Harton was preparing for his inaugural year at West View, cousin Charles Jr., his Uncle Charles Sr., and Ed Vettel oversaw the entire construction process until the start of the 1946 season. With the new ride additions, Harton established a naming contest for the new miniature railroad. The winning name for the new ride was Fledgling Flyer. Ruth Bodecker of suburban Dormont sent in the winning entry and was awarded a $100 savings bond by George Harton. The 1946 season marked West View Park's most successful year on record and marked the beginning of what would be the golden years.

When the Fledging Flyer debuted, gas pumps were installed and located at the back of the train station.

West View Park – The Golden Years Begin

With support from Brady McSwigan of Kennywood, Harton was named to the NAAPPB awards committee for 1947. This committee nominated individuals and issued service awards to organization members within the industry based on their leadership and service. Like his cousin before him, George Harton played an active role at the organization's yearly convention by presenting topics of interest to industry leaders and owners.

Harton followed 1946 by making annual improvements to the park for twenty years. What started as infrastructure improvements eventually turned into introducing new rides. Starting in 1946, West View Park guests began to see the number of attractions grow. Harton relied heavily on Ed Vettel's expertise to further design and develop the backside of the property near the Racing Whippet and on the hill near the athletic field and dance pavilion.

A young family is eager to take a ride on the Tilt-a-Whirl

With a family of his own, Harton decided to add multiple children's rides for the growing population of young families.

This began the era of a strong partnership between West View Park and the Allan Herschell Company. The Allan Herschell Company dates back to the late 1800s, just like the T.M. Harton Company. Allan Herschell, founder of the Allan Herschell Company, began his company by selling and manufacturing carousels. Successor companies were later created but, eventually, all Herschell-related companies merged back into one company. With the baby boom occurring, the Allan Herschell Company manufactured a number of kiddie rides, many of which are still in operation and popular with children today. The company also played a pivotal role in assisting West View Park in developing Kiddieland, making it a distinct area off the main midway.

Kiddieland was introduced in the early 1950s. The concept of Kiddieland, a complete miniature park within a park for young children, was envisioned by F.W. Henninger. Created at Kennywood for the 1927 season, Henninger

established what eventually became an industry standard and fixture in parks all over the country. Prior to Kiddieland being established at West View Park, children's attractions were scattered at the back end of the park, toward the Racing Whippet.

Following the end of World War II, the baby boomer generation entered the world. More than ever, West View Park emphasized its advertising strategies on being a fantastic entertainment destination for families. In a way to increase market awareness and generate positive publicity, the park introduced "Free Kiddie Days. Children from one to thirteen could ride all amusements free, with the ponies, water scooter boats, and Loop-o-Plane being the only exceptions. The promotion ran from 1 to 7 p.m. and was held twice a year. Park management estimated 5,000 children visited the park each Free Kiddie Day. In addition, the park entertained orphans three days a season free of charge, which included providing free meals and entertainment. When including public or private schools, church, community, and industrial picnics, park management estimated between 150,000 and 200,000 children attended. Management believed the park served as a healthy and commendable recreation location for children, teenagers, adults, and families.

"As a child growing up in the city, I looked forward to the yearly school picnics at West View Park. My mom would pack a basket and my dad would bring it up to the church where it would be picked up and delivered to the park by truck. The families would then board the trolley cars; they are the cars that ran on rails, and we settled in for the long ride to the park. As we rode along, we sang together and cheered our driver in anticipation of the fun day ahead. Upon arrival at the park, we located the pavilion where the food baskets were being held and secured a spot where we would later stop to eat. It was so exciting being in the park, riding the many rides, being with friends and eating cotton candy. When it was time to go home, we left thinking about next year, when we would spend another day at the park.

As I grew older, my girlfriend and I attended dances at West View Park Danceland. It was a beautiful building with a revolving mirror ball hanging from the ceiling that reflected beautiful colors around the room. There were live bands, and singer Bobby Vinton sang with his dad's band that played there often. Many couples met at the dances and later married. I met my husband there over 60 years ago. I treasure a photo taken there of my parents holding four of their grandchildren in front of the pony ride. Thanks for the memories, West View Park."

–Mary Alioto, Gibsonia, PA

This picnic area was located on the hill behind the administration office. It was also the location fireworks were shot off from.

George Harton developed the marketing strategy for West View Park and always looked for ways to keep the West View Park name in the newspapers. Many parks adopted directional arrows for automobile travelers and it soon became common practice. Many of the arrows pointed to the right while select arrows pointed to the left. The arrows were placed on telephone poles and featured a red arrow with white script spelling out West View Park. Meyers Lake Amusement Park in Canton, Ohio, used the same directional arrows as West View Park until Meyers Lake closed in 1974. To this day, Kennywood still utilizes directional arrows, which became a symbol for the park. As his son Dr. George Harton IV explained:

"Dad didn't just lead by spending money but believed the reinvestment; spending money and introducing something new every year was an essential part of customer retention. He was ahead of his time on customer retention. Even in tough years, Dad was committed to new, but especially returning, customers and motivated them to visit West View Park."

Introducing Danceland & WPGH

Harton introduced new improvements in 1947, including an extensive renovation of the park's administration office, a new radio tower, and a renovation of the dance pavilion. Renovations to the dance pavilion occurred in 1947, with major renovations occurring again in 1948. With the renovation came a new name: Danceland—a name used by multiple parks at the time. Fred Pearce used the name for his dance hall at Excelsior Amusement Park in Excelsior, Minnesota. Redesigned by Edward Vettel Sr. and constructed by three members of the Vettel family, the newly air-conditioned ballroom quickly became one of Pittsburgh's most popular music and stage venues.

Officially reopening on May 17, 1948, the 178 by 123 feet dancehall could accommodate 3,000 people. The huge air-conditioned West View Park ballroom proved so popular, President and General Manager George Harton quickly decided Danceland should operate on a year-round basis and explained:

> "We hope to cater to parties, banquets, college, and high school dances. We have just the right location and the proper atmosphere to give the Pittsburgh community just what it needs and wants."

The $250,000 renovations invested in Danceland proved to be a smart business decision. Surrounding the dance floor were tables and chairs that were moveable in the event the crowds demanded more room. In the rear of the building was a snack bar. The interior of the building was also decorated with a lighting system that featured fifty different lighting combinations, making for a remarkable dance experience. And located outside the main door were two large parking lots, just forty feet from the streetcar line. These parking lots provided supplemental access to accommodate the growing number of Pittsburghers who owned automobiles.

Jack "Jackie" Weisser, who at a young age worked at West View Park's original open-air dance pavilion, returned to work at the park upon his return from serving in the armed forces during WWII. Weisser worked as Jack Stoll's assistant; promoting, advertising, and bringing in bands to perform at Danceland. He worked on booking clubs and private events for Pittsburgh area college students from Pitt, Duquesne, and Carnegie Tech. According to

Weisser, Danceland hosted up to 3,000 patrons, if not more, on multiple occasions. Weisser said:

> "The record was held by Tex Benecke and the Glenn Miller Orchestra—2,941 people. But broadcasting the Chesterfield Hour coast-to-coast from the ballroom, the Ralph Flanagan Orchestra beat that record with 2,942."

During this period, Stoll and Weisser established their reputation and established Danceland as one of the nation's best dance centers. Just as he did with Danceland and at George Harton's request, Ed Vettel Sr. redesigned and enlarged the existing administration office to accommodate the growing middle management team. Harton inherited a fantastic middle management team from the Beares era that included Ed Vettel Sr., Ed Vettel Jr., Bob "Bud" Vettel, John Hickey, Howard "Ky" Howell, and park artist Jack Nofsinger.

The outdated dance pavilion was redesigned and reopened in 1948 as Danceland

George Harton III foresaw the marketing power a new dance pavilion could have on attracting patrons and families to the park.

Danceland brought in significant year round revenue to the park.

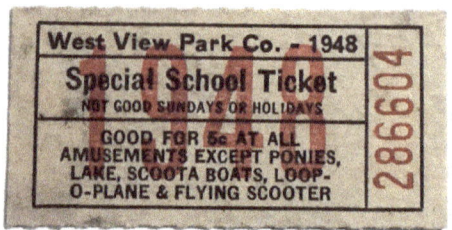 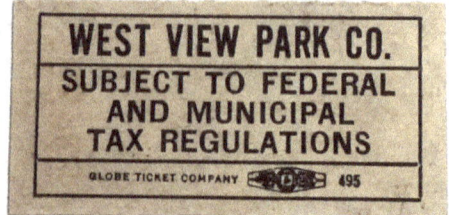

1948 West View Park Special School Ride Ticket

On the wall behind George Harton's desk was a painting of a carousel horse. When Nofsigner started working at the park in his early teens, he started out by selling tickets and later working midway games. His interest in drawing led him to design and create numerous projects and signs throughout the park. One particular project he was fond of was painting a mural for the park's shooting gallery. In the background were Native Americans, cowboys, and scenery. The murals created the environment of the Old West and captured park guests' imaginations. As a way to say thank you for being offered the opportunity to create a mural, Nofsinger painted then park General Manager Charles Beares Jr. as one of the cowboys riding a horse. Recognizing Nofsinger's artistic abilities, Harton tasked him to design the park's newspaper advertisements.

> "George was very nice. He was always interested in the park and was meant to work in the business,"
>
> *- Jack Nofsinger.*

A new business opportunity presented itself in 1947 when the FCC assigned the call letters for Pittsburgh's seventh radio station, WPGH 1080 AM. The station was originally operated by the Pittsburgh Broadcast Company; George Harton was one of the founding partners and a member of the Board of Directors. Garrett Richter, another member of the Board, was a close friend of George's from their days at Shadyside Academy and Princeton. After Harton's years in the Navy, Richter remained close friends with Harton, even introducing George to his future wife, Lillian. Richter eventually became involved in local and state government and was elected as a Representative for Allegheny County. In 1947, he presented a trophy to the winner of the Junior Miss Western Pennsylvania Pageant, which was held at West View Park. Richter was also the godfather of George's first child and daughter, Janet. By January 1950, WPGH changed ownership for a third time, with Harton maintaining majority control (49 percent) with William Zeuger and Garrett Richter. Walter Fenker, who was recently appointed secretary and assistant treasurer at West View Park, was appointed to the same position with WPGH. The following year, Harton bought out his two partners, officially making him sole owner.

Garrett Richter and G.M. Harton III awarding the winner of the 1947 Junior Miss Western Pennsylvania Pageant

The radio station served as a means for Harton to become an active investor in outside business opportunities as well as provide an easier avenue to actively promote West View Park. In 1954, Harton sold the radio station, which was renamed 1080 WILY.

By the 1940s, the second generation of Vettels emerged as individuals interested in working in the amusement industry. Cousins Ed and Andrew Vettel were roommates at the University of Alabama while studying electrical engineering. Andrew graduated in 1936 and Ed Jr. graduated in 1938.

Andrew joined his father, Erwin, at Kennywood, while Ed joined his father, Edward, at West View Park. Ed took on the position of assistant superintendent in 1949 after spending almost ten years traveling and constructing rides. When asked why he entered the amusement industry for a June 23, 1947, article in the *Pittsburgh Post-Gazette*, Edward E. Vettel explained:

> "I don't know when I decided to go into the amusement construction business—we call them gravity rides. There wasn't any certain point. I suppose I just drifted into it—gravity, you might call [it]."

By this time, Kennywood's three roller coasters began to show their age. Kennywood hired Ed Vettel, Sr. as a consultant to assess them and recommend the necessary work needed so that the roller coasters would remain in top operating condition. With the work came an eventual rebuild of the Racer in 1949 and new Ed Vettel, Sr.-designed trains for the Jack Rabbit in 1951. Ed Sr. made several trips to Kennywood to consult on roller coaster maintenance and provided notes to his nephew Andrew.

Following his father's death in 1943, Andrew Vettel, better known as Andy Vettel Sr., continued to run a highly respected maintenance department as park superintendent at Kennywood. Not satisfied with his job, testing electrical motors at Westinghouse Electric upon graduating from the University of Alabama, Andy Vettel Sr. began working part-time at Kennywood at the suggestion of his father. Andy Vettel's father, Erwin Vettel, began his tenure at Kennywood in March 1936, when, with the help of his brother Ed, accepted the position of mechanical superintendent, replacing Charles Mach, who retired. Andy Sr. was known as a talented draftsman. To this day, and through the skills and knowledge that were passed down through his successor, Fred Weber, Kennywood's safety record has remained strong. In 1954, Fred Weber joined the Kennywood maintenance department full time, and together with Andy Vettel Sr., the two developed a strong working relationship. While Vettel wasn't entirely hands-on, Weber could do and fix anything. The two men developed one of the safest and most respected maintenance programs in the amusement industry.

Interestingly enough, Andy Vettel Sr. maintained a residence inside Kennywood, something that was quite common back in that day for amusement park employees across the country. The residence at Kennywood happened to be the same house his parents lived in upon moving to Kennywood in 1936. During his tenure at Kennywood, Andy Vettel designed two roller coasters: The Dipper and Thunderbolt. Beginning as the Little Dipper in 1948, this junior coaster was later lengthened (by 440 feet) and redesigned in 1950 and 1955. The ride was removed in 1983 to make way for the Raging Rapids.

In 1949, the last new Ed Vettel-designed roller coaster opened at West View Park. Because the junior coaster was popular at Kennywood, it may have been the reason for building and introducing the Kiddie Dips at West View. The ride featured Ed Vettel-designed trains with safety lock bars. The loading platform structure was fronted by evergreens and plenty of neon lights. In an announcement through *The Billboard* in the June 18, 1949 issue, George Harton said:

"The junior ride has adult as well as kid appeal."

The Vettels were very active at both West View Park and Kennywood. While competitors, both parks embodied the spirit and philosophy of the amusement industry of helping each other out and determining best safety and operational standards. Kathy Vettel, daughter of Bob Vettel and a third generation Vettel family member to work at West View Park explained:

"Although they were competitors, West View and Kennywood were family. It wasn't a job, it was family. West View Park was gorgeous. It was smaller than Kennywood, but it was beautiful. Just like Kennywood, the park had a natural landscape but West View had the hills and terrain.

West View Park wasn't just an amusement park to me. It was an extension of my home and family and part of my daily life as I was growing up. I remember eating dinner in the dining room at the cafeteria with my father when working at the park; I worked at Fascination.

West View Park was my 'home' away from home for 18 years. Everyone knew who my father and grandfather were. Even once I started college in North Carolina, I came home to Pittsburgh every summer and worked at the park to make money for college expenses. I recall Dad and I singing crazy songs and laughing riding to the park together in his red Jeep going to work.

West View Park and the Vettel name went hand in hand. After all, every time I rode the Big Dips, I was proud to see my grandfather's name and it reminded me of what a special engineer and person he was to have had the knowledge to do what he did as a profession. How many people can say their grandfather designed or built roller coasters for a living—HOW COOL IS THAT!!! I'll never forget the Big Dips. That first drop was breathtaking."

Kathy Vettel Hilton – Meadville, PA

In December 1950, business and office-related work was streamlined when the T.M. Harton Company moved its headquarters to West View Park from downtown Pittsburgh, one of the many long-term goals established by T.M. Harton when West View Park opened.

In the early part of the 1900s, and for years after, it was very common for parks and other businesses to have a centralized headquarters located in downtown Pittsburgh. Not only did this serve as a common central location for meetings, it was more convenient for mail de-

Kathy Vettel with her dog Duke, in front of her father's West View Park Jeep

livery. Until the development of long-distance phone calls and the internet, park owners and managers sent letters as a means to share best practices and address other issues.

Public Relations & Marketing Strategies

Since becoming President and General Manager, Harton insisted on strong public relations and marketing. At the 1949 industry convention in Chicago, Harton had his public relations director, Harry Kodinsky, speak on the subject. Kodinsky explained how public relations is far from being seasonal and should operate on a year-round basis. The forum also discussed the importance of becoming involved with the community and telling the public what goes on behind the scenes. Kodinsky spoke from an honest point of view. Most people believe that once an amusement park closes for the season, employees take long vacations and/or do very little during the off-season. In reality, any amusement park's off-season is just as busy. Management is constantly looking at ways to improve overall operations and, more importantly, better the guest experience.

The guest experience encompassed everything West View could offer. Free entertainment held at the free act stage and Talkie Temple were a big part of the marketing strategy. Entertainment was one of the driving factors

The Talkie Temple was known to have large crowds throughout the summer. The Talkie Temple also helped attract guests to visit the park, simply for the free entertainment.

that brought guests to West View Park. The park booked most of its entertainment through George A. Hamid, known throughout the industry as the owner and operator of Atlantic City's famous Steel Pier and George Hamid General Amusements booking agency. Similar to Hamid, George Harton owned and operated his own booking agency in the late 1940s to early 1950s. In 1949, George Harton was actively seeking flying, aerial, and animal acts for West View Park when George Keller answered the ad. For years, the agency represented Billy Outten and his high diving act. The George M Harton Agency booked entertainment for parks, fairs, and expositions.

Billy Outten and his family were frequent performers at the park.

Free act shows were always a hit with children, and George Keller and his wild animals became a yearly show. Once the park season was in full tilt and operating daily by the end of May, free shows at the Talkie Temple and free act stage began. Professor George Keller and his wild animals performed twice a day. Each summer, he opened his tour of shows at West View Park. Keller performed with circuses, at theatres, fairs, and at amusement parks such as West View, Conneaut Lake, Olympic Park in New Jersey,

Professor George Keller was another popular act brought to the park annually.

Carlin's Park in Baltimore, and Rocky Point Park in Warick, Rhode Island. George J. Keller's Jungle Killers was billed as America's Finest Wild Animal Act. Keller began performing at West View in the 1940s. A college professor, Keller was always fascinated by wild animals and eventually stepped away from teaching to focus on his animal act. Each year, he exhibited his growing collection of trained cats and remained a popular entertainer until his final show at the park in 1960.

Big Bands & The Baby Boom

Instead of only focusing on new rides, Harton also began focusing on games as a source of generating revenue. Not only did patrons visit for the rides, but guests now came to play games. A new game called Fascination made its debut at the park in the early 1950s. One of the most popular games ever installed and played at the park, Fascination remained a game staple at the park and in the amusement industry for years to come.

Danceland, which provided a great deal of revenue, began hosting celebration galas to large crowds, the most popular of which were the parties held on New Year's Eve. Tickets and reservations were a must, and year after year, Pittsburghers looked forward to the annual event. Many bands and entertainers performed at these galas. Bob Vettel and his wife, Arlene, worked the New Year's Eve parties at Danceland. The Vettels spent every New Year at Danceland cooking, preparing, and running the event. This was also the era when big bands such as Lee Kelton, Lee Barrett, Ralph Flanagan, Guy Lombardo, and Louis Prima performed at the park. When Guy Lombardo played at Danceland on September 8, 1951, the band drew 1,656 patrons.

Danceland was a popular location for dates, and was where many Pittsburgh couples met.

In 1952, George Harton was elected to serve a two-year term as president of the Pennsylvania Amusement Park Association. During this time, many park operators were apprehensive about the years ahead, as owners/operators did not want to price themselves out of business. Operating costs started to increase in the 1950s. Taxes hampered parks in raising prices to keep step with inflation. Admission prices to individual rides at West View Park had remained the same as they were in the late 1930s.

In 1953, West View Park experienced its first season without Park Superintendent Ed Vettel Sr., as he unexpectantly passed away in November 1952. Since the park's first days, Vettel Sr. played a vital role in the design and construction process of every project at the park. While it was difficult for management to carry on without him, the maintenance department was left in the trusted hands of Vettel's two sons. Ed Vettel Jr. was named superintendent and Bob "Bud" Vettel was named assistant superintendent. Prior to working in the amusement industry, Bud served in the Army Air Force in Europe during World War II. After returning home, he began working at West View alongside his brother and father. He not only assisted in

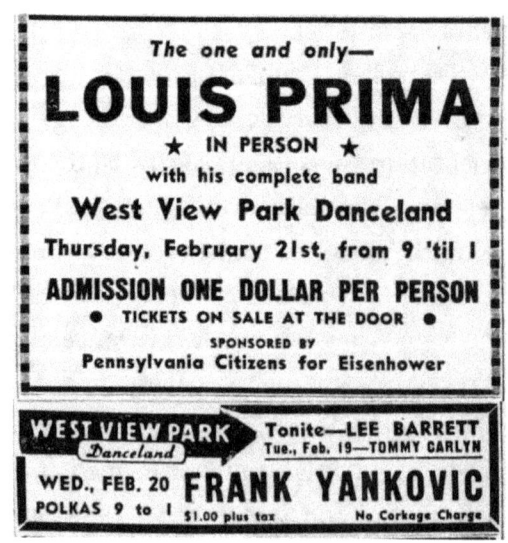

maintaining rides but also was the refrigeration engineer; he designed and installed heating and cooling units inside many of the park's buildings. According to Bud's daughter Kathy, her father was proud to work at West View and continue his father's legacy:

> "It wasn't a job to him, it was family, and he loved that park. He worked 24/7 in the summer. He installed the heating and cooling for the cafeteria and Bavarian Room and in George Harton's house on the hill. The only thing I remember was the Baby Grand Piano in the home."

In the 1950s, George Harton had a house built that was constructed by the Vettels and other park personnel on the property purchased from West View Park Company. The roof featured Italian clay tiles, stone fireplaces, a three-car garage, a billiard room, wine cellar, seven bedrooms, and nine bathrooms. During the Christmas season, Harton would take extra carousel reindeer figures out of storage and place them in his front yard, situated next to a blue spruce tree. Lit up by two flood-lights, the scene was a well-known community attraction, as passing cars slowed down to look at the festive yard decorations every holiday season. The house, located on Bellevue Road in West View, still stands and is now the North Hills Free Methodist Church.

West View Park Celebrates 50 Years

West View Park celebrated its 50th anniversary in 1955 and looked forward to many more years of expansion and successful operations. More than 500 picnics were held at West View Park, and about 500 individuals found employment during peak operating months. The park had always been known for its lights at night, and just like all of the parks in the country, the lights created magic under the night stars. Concluding each day that year was what West View Park called the Winter Carnival. It was an all-season-long event that featured a large parade down the midway with giant inflated figures, floats, and bands. The festivities were very similar to Kennywood's annual Fall Fantasy Parade. Performing that season were some of the best dance orchestras in the Tri-State along with name bands such as Billy May, Vaughn Monroe, Tommy and Jimmy Dorsey, Less Brown, Tex Beneke, Ray Anthony, and Woody

Parades were common in the evening during the parks 50th anniversary season

Herman. By 1955, Harton was looking to add a new mixture of attractions to the park. While manufacturers in the United States exported attractions, Europe began exporting attractions to the United States. The latest industry trend was to install rides imported from Europe. Conklin Shows of Ontario, Canada, was one of the largest importers of European rides and communicated frequently with park owners and managers throughout the United States.

Both European flat rides and roller coasters were being introduced and installed at parks at a gradual pace. Initially, markets were limited with certain European rides and how many could operate within a certain radius. The Rotor, marketed as the World's Latest and Greatest Sensation when it debuted in England, was initially sold under this stipulation. While on a park tour in Europe in October 1955, Harton contacted Chas Freeman, director of Rotor Dromes Limited and manufacturers of the Rotor. During their meeting, Harton expressed interest in wanting to sign a deal for a new Rotor at West View Park. To his disappointment, Freeman informed Harton that because a Rotor was in operation at nearby Kennywood Park, installing and operating the same attraction at West View Park was out of question. Although he was disappointed, Harton continued his tour of Europe by visiting the Thompson family at Blackpool Pleasure Beach and later Spain.

The quest for installing a Rotor at West View Park never ended and eventually a Rotor made a late season appearance at the park in the late 1950s. Janet Von Twistern explained the ride was a late addition one summer season, and her father had WIIC Channel 11 film a promotion featuring the Rotor. Another attraction added to West View based on an attraction found in Europe was the Haunted Swing in 1956. This attraction was an optical illusion to make riders believe they were being flipped upside-down.

Changes on The Horizon

In 1957, Walbridge Park, one of the few remaining subsidiary business units of the T.M. Harton Company, closed. Dwindling attendance, along with social and cultural changes, forced the company to shutter the park. According to Charles Beares III, Walbridge Park never had the parking space for automobiles like West View Park did, and for that reason, it was never "a real moneymaker." The T.M. Harton Company formally dissolved the Walbridge

WALBRIDGE PARK AMUSEMENT CENTER, TOLEDO, OHIO—7

Shortly after assuming the role of President role of T.M. Harton Company, George Harton appointed Snyder Custer, GM of Walbridge Park, a position he held until the park closed in 1957.

Park Amusement Company on December 23, 1959, after all assets were sold or relocated to West View Park. The company received several offers to purchase the land the park land in Toledo, Ohio.

The City of Toledo challenged the company, and the sale of the property was put on hold. Eventually, the city purchased the property after seven years of discussion. Once the sale was completed in June of 1964, the T.M. Harton Company now owned a single company: West View Park.

The late 1950s were marked by dramatic industry changes for regional parks due to the opening of Disneyland in 1955. Initially, amusement industry leaders resisted Walt Disney's concept of bringing themes to parks and did not foresee people traveling long distance to visit Disneyland; however, Walt Disney countered by saying that people would travel long distance to Disneyland since automobiles were becoming more common and impacted how people traveled. Walt Disney consulted and befriended many leaders within the industry. One such person was Ed Schott, park owner of Coney Island in Cincinnati, who provided Disney with the guidance and consulting he needed to make Disneyland the finest run operation. The comradery of helping others within the amusement industry proved critical to the success of Disneyland.

According to Janet Von Twistern, daughter of George Harton III, her father was one of the individuals within the amusement industry who agreed that Walt Disney and Disney Imagineering would transform the industry and bring about exciting changes. According to Janet, her father traveled to California frequently to meet with Disney to discuss Disneyland and the future of Disney Theme Parks. He first became friends with Walt Disney through his involvement as a Board member with the NAAPPB. Harton vacationed in Fort Lauderdale, Florida, every spring, and in the late 1950s, while on vacation, he conceived the idea of building his own amusement park there. Harton was serious enough about the idea that he looked into purchasing land for his project, but he began to encounter health issues that stemmed from his time in the military, and while the idea seemed grand, he realized he did not have the funds to undertake a project of that size.

Janet explained that when the opportunity came, her father shared pictures and data with Walt Disney and explained that Florida would be a successful market for a park and plenty of undeveloped land was available. Eventually, Walt Disney liked the idea enough that he decided the next Disney Theme Park would be built in Florida.

Not only was Harton focused on the future of the industry and eager to see Walt Disney succeed, he was also focused on finalizing his ten-year plan for West View Park. In the late 1950s and early 1960s, picnics and events continued to grow at West View Park. Starting in 1956, the park started hosting the Pittsburgh Pirates for a day each season. Players had access to the rides during the day and in the evening, and the players and their families enjoyed a complimentary dinner at Danceland. Not only were guests excited to meet their favorite players, they were also excited to meet their families.

While Harton was known throughout West View Borough, the same can be said about his Irish Wolfhound dog, Boru. West View Park never introduced a mascot character, but for a time, Boru fit that role. George Harton leveraged his own dog as a marketing tool for the park. Boru was also a hit with the children. When walking the park, George Harton would take Boru with him and greet the park guests, especially young children. His son explained:

"Dad was always encouraging photos to be taken with Boru and have it sent to the newspapers."

Bob Friend and Gino Cimoli of the Pittsburgh Pirates, visit with a group of young fans in West View Park's Danceland

G.M. Harton III is seen with his dog Boru greeting a young guest

When Boru was at the park, but not on the midway, he could be found sitting next to his best friend on the second story of the luxurious administrative building, in the grand size living room George Harton called his office. This is where Harton worked and was able to keep a watchful eye on the park. Even when he was home, Harton was known to stand in front of his picture window counting the cars at Danceland. Behind the wide desk was George's big red leather swivel chair, and in the one corner was a sofa covered in green fabric, with a large coffee table in front of it. In front of his desk, in a wide 25-foot arc, were ten armchairs covered in green, yellow, and red leather. Each chair represented a department at the park for meetings held during or after business hours. The entire office was soundproof, including two soundproof picture windows that looked out across the park. Within the wood wall was a refrigerator and a speaker connected to the park's radio tower, television, record player, and microphone. As Dr. George Harton IV recalled, there was even a poker table:

> "When I'd visit, I got invited to play poker with Dad's poker buddies who worked at the park. I don't remember what the stakes were. It was for money."

Known to stay until late at night, Harton would always be the last to leave for the day, if he left at all. Like many park owners and managers of the day, Harton also had an apartment at the park where he frequently stayed. His apartment was located at his office in the administration building, which featured sleeping quarters. He also had an office at Danceland located at the front of the building behind the block window. This office featured an office, furniture and signed pictures lined on the walls, of bands or entertainers that performed at the park. Harton was the definition of a dedicated park leader and employee. Always presenting himself in a professional manner, George Harton, the blonde-haired and sharply dressed general manager, knew he had finally found his calling in life by living his dream of doing what was started by his uncle and father. Displayed prominently in his office in the administration building were photographs of his Uncle T.M., and father, George. Ironically, he always encouraged his children to find their calling by saying, "If you can do something you love, you will never work." This ultimately became one of the reasons West View Park closed.

The administration building also hosted offices for other members of management, including Jack Stoll, who managed Danceland, Assistant Picnic Managers Larry Robey and John "Jack" Hickey Jr., and Advertising and Marketing Manager Alan Leonard. Leonard was also tasked with designing the Bavarian Room added in 1954. He hired artists to paint murals inside from postcards he purchased in Bavaria. In addition, he also designed George's office. Margaret and Harry Habel's daughter, Carol Mcilvan, recalled:

> "Alan Leonard had an eye for the artistic side of things … decorating in general. George (Harton) and Alan would go to New York City to shop when they refurbished the president's office in the main building and when Danceland was redone. George had an office there."

If park meetings were not held in the administration office, they were held in a private conference room called the committee room, behind the main Bavarian Room tavern or Beer Garden. The Bavarian Room was more modern than the cafeteria. It was one of the first building's people would pass on the midway from the main entrance parking lot off Route 19. The older cafeteria

The Bavarian Room was a large, themed Beer Garden. Unlike many parks at the time, West View Park sold alcohol. Today, most parks in the amusement industry sell alcohol at their facility

was a typical dine-in area where basic meals were prepared daily, as were specials for each operating day. Elizabeth Ruh was the cafeteria manager from 1906 until her retirement in 1952. According to Charles Beares III, Ruh was a very loyal long-term employee, known as "Uncle Marsh's first hire for West View Park." Margaret Patinni, a longtime and loyal park employee, was the cafeteria supervisor. When the Harton family or upper management would use the private dining room in the cafeteria, Patinni was known to take orders and serve the food. Former West View Park employee Al Seitz recalled:

> "I was not hired at first, but a good friend of mine was hired in the cafeteria and recommended me to the cafeteria supervisor, Margaret Pattini, and she hired me directly. My primary job was busboy, which was great, since we were out in the dining area all day. The cafeteria pies were brought in from a bakery that I do not recall now, but they were the best! Every night when we closed, we prepped for the next day, [and] every chair was wiped and put seat down on the tables, so that we could mop the floor. We cleaned the kitchen as well. No one went home until the place was in inspection order. We were like a family at the cafeteria, Margaret was firm but fair."

West View Park and the T.M. Harton Company continued to be a family run and operated business. T.M. Harton Company officers other than President George Harton III included Vice President Dick F. Newman (George Harton III's uncle), Vice President A.E. Kountz (George Harton III's stepfather), Treasurer Carice Kountz (George Harton III's mother), and Secretary and Assistant Treasurer Walter Fenker. Working close, on the second floor of the administration building, was Margaret Habel, George Harton III's executive secretary. She began working at West View in 1935, at the age of 18, when hired by Charles Beares II as a money counter; she later worked for George Harton III. During the mid-1950s, George Harton's daughter, Janet, began working as Margaret's assistant.

Janet wore multiple hats and worked in many office capacities. Since she worked with Habel, she was able to learn a lot about the park's business affairs. Janet thoroughly enjoyed her job during the summers, and her father was looking to transition her into a larger role with the T.M. Harton Company and West View Park. In addition, Walter Fenker, the secretary and assistant treasurer, worked with Habel managing the finances of the T.M. Harton

George Harton IV and Janet Harton are pictured here enjoying a marathon of repeat rides on the Racing Whippet.

Company and West View Park Company. Habel, was a highly trusted employee of George Harton's and worked with him on many projects.

The administration building, which housed the cashier's office, managed by Helen Ollife, was the location where employees received their pay in cash every two weeks. This was also the location where employees could purchase refreshment tickets at a discounted price, which could be used to purchase food at the refreshment stands. Carol Mcilvan said:

> "Helen Olliffe was in charge of the money counting room on the first floor on the main office building. She dealt with all the booth cashiers selling ride tickets up and down the midway. She took care of the bank deposits for the daily receipts."

Loyal Career Staff

Park carpenter and roller coaster veteran Ivan Murray started with the T.M. Harton Company around 1920. He traveled the country helping to build coasters for the company and for the Vettels. Then in 1935, he returned to West View Park as one of the lead carpenters. Because he built roller coasters, every morning, Murray walked the entire course of West View's roller coasters to inspect the rides for loose spikes, rails, boards, and any other maintenance concerns.

Another loyal member of the staff was Frank Martin. He started his years of employment at West View in 1948. Originally arriving at West View with his trailer to live in, Martin took care of the park's twenty ponies.

Margaret and Harry Habel, Jack Weisser, Helen Olliffe, and Walter Fenker

The ponies gave approximately 100,000 children a single ride each summer season. Many girls obtained their first job through Martin, because he believed girls worked better with children and the ponies. Prior to opening for the day, the employees who worked at the pony track would ride and exercise the ponies before children would ride them. Martin provided each pony with a name, taught them tricks, and had them perform the tricks for the children.

During the summer, Martin lived in his trailer, next to the pony track, and also managed the park's greenhouse. Originally, the greenhouse was not part of his job duties, but he believed West View Park could always use more flowers and landscaping, so he started the greenhouse to keep West View a well-landscaped amusement park. Martin also maintained gardens where he grew strawberries and other vegetables. From its inception, West View Park management continued the vision of T.M. Harton, where trees, landscaping, and undeveloped property was part of the ambiance of the property.

Not only were there great lower-level employees at the park, there were additional key members of the West View Park management team. Some of the park's faithful employees included Alex Nagy and Charles "Good Cakes" Smedley, who helped to maintain a family spirit among the staff. Nagy oversaw ground maintenance and was known to be able to fix anything. These employees and many others became family to the Hartons and were treated as such. The family atmosphere was evident due to the Harton family but also because of the multiple generations of the Vettel and Hickey families

Frank Martin managed the parks Pony Track for many years. Riders of all ages enjoyed riding the ponies.

The 1946 park expansion designed by Ed Vettel Sr and Charlie Beares Jr made an immediate impact by increasing revenue and attendance

working at West View. The Hickey's were largely assisted by Harry Habel who called and visited local school districts, booking picnics. By the late 1950s, Ed "Boots" Vettel, a third generation Vettel, and son of Ed Jr., began working at West View as a ride operator driving the miniature train. Cousin Andy Vettel's children, Erwin, Dorothy, and later Andy Jr., also began working in the industry at crosstown competitor Kennywood.

New Strategies & Challenges

John Hickey Sr. and John "Jack" Hickey Jr. worked diligently to grow the picnic business at West View Park. School picnics were the lifeblood of the park's revenue in the months of May and June, but by July, picnics transitioned into industrial, union, and community or heritage/ethnic group picnics. The Carpenters Union picnic and Mellon Bank picnic were two of the largest annual picnics held at West View. The Teamsters Union and Polish Community picnics were very popular and heavily attended.

WVP Vice President Dick Newman, President and GM George Harton III, and Picnic Manager John Hickey Sr.

"Each year, a neighbor, Mr. Kegal, would take all the kids with most of their fathers to West View Park for the all-day Teamsters (Truck Drivers Union) picnic. We piled into three or four big cars in those days to travel to the park. Some men took their younger children on rides because most rides had a colored height scale on the wall next to where you bought ride tickets. If you were too short, you needed an adult to go with you. All rides were free, compliments of the Teamsters. When we ran out, we walked back to the Talkie Temple area and looked for our neighbor, who constantly had more tickets to give to anyone in our group. Here is the last great part of the great free day at West View: our dads or Mr. Kegal would give us a quarter or half dollar we would use to go to the Penny Arcade and spend hours there."

John Andra – Pittsburgh, PA

Throughout July and August weekdays, when picnics were not scheduled, West View initiated Thorofare Days. Thorofare was a local grocery supermarket chain founded in Pittsburgh. Tickets could be purchased at any Thorofare location, and this new marketing campaign helped attract business and increase attendance.

The steel strike of 1959 hurt amusement parks located in the country's rust belt region. Parks such as West View, Kennywood, Conneaut Lake, Idora in Youngstown, and Meyers Lake in Canton, Ohio, struggled through that summer season. By August 17, a settlement had yet to be reached, and owners were hopeful the labor issues would be resolved the following year. While West View's rides had a drastic decline from the previous year in revenue, business held up well for Danceland. Industrial picnics were pivotal for many parks, and as manufacturing—most notably the steel industry—declined, many parks lost picnics. Once these picnics were lost, some parks were unable to continue operating. Parks such as West View and Kennywood were able to continue due to location and the large number of businesses and working-class people. Pittsburgh had always been home to many businesses, especially large corporations like United States Steel, J&L Steel, Koppers, Alcoa, Gulf Oil, Mellon Bank, Westinghouse, WABCO, and H.J. Heinz. Business at West View in the 1950s was strong, and it was estimated that revenue was over one million dollars in its three and a half summer month operating window. In addition to all of the groups, schools, companies, and organizations, there were also many loyal guests, such as Joe Marasti.

"My wife and I did indeed frequent West View in the 50s and 60s. When I was an altar boy in the middle 50s at Mary Immaculate on the North Side, several of us would hop on the East Street streetcar and ride to West View to ride the Dips, and then return before lunch hour had concluded. We had 1 hour, 15 minutes for lunch each day, and in late May, when the park had opened, we took advantage of comp tickets that our priest, Fr. Dom Oliver, passed on to us. Fun times for sure. My wife, who was two years behind me at Mary Immaculate, also made many trips to West View before and after we were married. Those trips began in 1963 following my discharge from the U.S. Navy and continued in our young married life until the park closed. We were also fortunate to get comp tickets from Joe Love, who was my dad's boss and a former mayor of West View. West View was a wonderful family park, and Danceland was a bonus to the young people who enjoyed the many bands that played there."

Joe Marasti, Sr. – Penn Township, PA

By 1960, George Harton was looking for new assistant managers as the park continued to grow. Originally hired as the West View public relations manager in May 1960, George Bodnar introduced the Over 19, Over 20, and Over 21 record dances at Danceland. The park also held Under 18 dances, with much success. Bodnar worked primarily at Danceland but was also West View's entertainment coordinator. He replaced Jack Weisser, who previously held an administrative leadership role at Danceland, assisting Jack Stoll.

"Somewhere around high school and then college graduation, my friends introduced me to Danceland. Suddenly, the park I didn't much care for became a magical place—Wednesdays and Fridays, for those nights of the teen dances! Picture this big crystal ball hanging in the center, throwing off light reflections like the stars, and some of the best recorded music of that day being piped through the sound system. For as much fun and for looking forward so much to those dances, I never called or dated a girl that I met and danced with. I'm not sure why, but for a young guy just getting familiar with the boy-girl world, Danceland was perfect for me."

Paul Ley – Dayton, OH

Assistant General Manager George Bodnar is seen here with two new figures waiting to be installed in the new Haunted House.

But by 1964, public dancing started losing its popularity. Bodnar and Harton decided it was best to allocate resources elsewhere in the park upon Jack Stoll's retirement and focus on utilizing Danceland for live entertainment, scaling back on public dances. From May 1944 through 1964, Jack Stoll had managed the West View Park dance pavilion. Starting at the park when the building was still an open-air ballroom, Stoll later became manager when Danceland was introduced. In a company letter dated December 2, 1964, George Harton had this to say about Stoll:

> "He has always been an honest, loyal, conscientious, and hardworking employee. We found him, as a manager, to have a salesman's personality with the customers, and his services [were] most satisfactory."

Although new to the management team, Bodnar's responsibilities began to grow each year. His son, George, even took on seasonal employment at the park. West View Park was truly a multi-generational family business. Because

Bodnar was performing well in his role, he and John "Jack" Hickey Jr. were named assistant manager and assistant general manager. Like his sister Janet, George Harton IV began being groomed for a leadership role. At 14 years of age, George IV began working at West View as a ticket counter in a building behind the miniature train station, where routine maintenance was completed on the train engines. He counted ride tickets and totaled up how much money each individual ride brought in each operating day. By the summer of 1962, he was assisting George Bodnar and working the shows at the free act stage and Talkie Temple.

Live performances also were still going strong at Danceland. Musical Artists such as Bobby Vinton, The Duprees, Tommy Roe, Florraine Darlin, Paul and Paula, Freddy "Boom Boom" Cannon, Stan Kenton, Tommy Carlin, the Skyliners, and the Four Freshman brought in large crowds. Park goer Chuck Brunner recalled seeing the Four Freshmen multiple times at Danceland and talking to the group members as they greeted fans between sets. Management signed a variety of artists to meet popular demand, and orchestras such as Barry Blue and Artie Arnell, jazz musicians Walt Harper and Harold Betters, and noted soul musician James Brown all performed at Danceland. Polka Nights were also popular, and Frank "Frankie" Yankovic performed multiple times, as did Frank Wojnarowksi and his nationally famous band.

Dr. George Harton IV fondly remembered "The Three Georges" (Dad, Bodnar, and me) traveling to numerous parks, particularly in Ohio and Minnesota, while he was in college (1961–1965). Traveling to other amusement parks was, and still remains, an important part of operating a successful amusement park. It provides an opportunity to see what is popular elsewhere and see how other park managers operate and overcome obstacles. West View management communicated and met frequently with other park owners and managers to discuss operating practices during and after each summer season.

The park owners included Brady McSwigan and the Henningers from Kennywood, the Freed family from Lagoon in Utah, the Schott and Wach family from Coney Island in Ohio, the Thompson family from Blackpool Pleasure Beach in England, and other regional park owners. As always, park owners and managers gathered and traveled to the International Association of Amusement Parks convention held every November. This tradition remains strong today.

The 1960s brought with it racial issues and incidents that were occurring in every park, and it proved to be a very segregated decade for the country. Like every park, West View Park encountered racial issues especially with admittance to Danceland. Park management discussed best practices with other owners and managers on how to handle these situations; however, not all parks succeeded. It was also during this time that the concept of pay one price entered the amusement industry. While many parks still relied on rides to make money via individual ride tickets, more and more parks began to implement a pay one price option for unlimited rides. As a business back then, the park was only open for three months, not year-round. While some parks started to move away from free entertainment, West View still actively booked major acts. The pay one price option allowed guests to save money and turn what was typically a half-day event into an entire day visit. As Janet Von Twistern said:

"My father was seriously considering going to pay one price only."

One price days and Thorofare days dominated the weekdays during the months of July and August. Separate stands were set up for guests to wait in line for a wristband and ride all day for just one price. The idea of seriously considering a single general admission accelerated when, in June 1961, an aerialist's pole collapsed during a show at the free act stage, killing a guest.

In the amusement industry, when incidents or accidents occur, lawsuits often ensue and park employees are often subpoenaed to testify in court. That was the case when Assistant General Manager George Bodnar, Park Superintendent Ed Vettel Jr., and Park Carpenter Robert Kummer had to testify during the court case. Fault for the accident attempted to place blame on the park, but the testimony by Bodnar, Vettel, and Kummer showed that the performer, not the park, was at fault for the incident. Although criminal charges and negligence were ruled out, a monetary settlement was negotiated.

Former West View Park employee Tom "Benny" Benson was at the park the day this accident occurred. He said he used to visit the park frequently for the free shows/acts and not spend a dollar during the day. After the accident, the shows went away, and as Tom said, and for another good reason, "The park did not make money off the shows." Wanting to eliminate the risk of another accident and increase revenue elsewhere in the park, the free shows/acts were eliminated. Since West View first opened free entertainment, it had always been an attendance draw, but moving forward, management elected to rely on the rise of amusements to attract patrons.

George Harton was willing to be the entrepreneur and focus less on free acts by only booking entertainment suited for the Talkie Temple. As television became more popular, the danger element in acts became less of a draw; however, Harton still wanted to develop a new hybrid business model that still incorporated entertainment. The new business model, which was met with immediate success, particularly in August, still incorporated previous models of entertainment and individual tickets. Relying less on entertainment accelerated the push for additional one price days during the operating season. Although the idea of offering a one price day option every day was attractive, like most parks, Harton elected to keep the hybrid two admission model. Interestingly enough, Kennywood would become solely a general admission park in 2005, replacing free admission and individual ride tickets.

To accommodate additional rides, a portion of the lake was filled in for the Wild Mouse to be installed.

Harton's Final Years

George Harton was known for being an aggressive decision maker. He was a forward thinker and willing to try new ideas that others thought were too risky at the time. Although exact plans and projects are unknown, it is believed Harton would have continued to embrace and participate in new industry trends; however, those dreams would not become reality.

In 1961, West View Park added the Wild Mouse roller coaster next to the Whip. Located on a section of lake that had been filled in, the ride was imported from Europe and operated under a concession basis, with the ride owner

West View Mayor Ted Benson is seen cutting the ribbon for the newly re-designed Kiddieland on Sunday, May 13, 1962.

and park splitting the profit earned from the attraction. Debuting in June of the same year was the 32-foot slide called the Magic Carpet. The following season saw the addition of the Krazy-Dazy Orbit, better known as the Scrambler, to the newly expanded midway. The ride was located next to the park's administration office. West View Park was also proud to boast what was now considered the largest Kiddieland in the country in 1962. Featuring nineteen rides and a pony track, the park redeveloped the area for a new generation and recognized the importance of progress. On hand to officially welcome and open the new Kiddieland was Captain Jim from TV's Channel 11 WIIC, President George Harton, and West View Borough Mayor Ted Benson (cutting the ribbon). Three-fourths of the yearly budget was spent on expanding and improving Kiddieland. This was also when an official Kiddieland entranceway sign was designed and built.

Kiddieland was home to numerous children attractions. The carousel pavilion in Kiddieland, originally held a full sized carousel through the 1930s but was eventually replaced by a W.F. Mangel's Kiddie Carousel and Pony Cart ride.

By installing the Antique Cars, West View Park solidified itself at the forefront of the industry of being early adopters to new ride concepts

The Wild Mouse was removed after the 1962 season to make way for a new theme park-styled ride, the Antique Cars. Manufactured by Arrow Development, the new ride was the first of its kind in the metro area and competing parks. West View was only the fourth park (Cedar Point, Freedomland USA, and Six Flags Over Texas were the others) to install a ride of this kind. The ride was also the first Arrow Development antique car ride to feature the 1911 Maxwell Touring car as ride vehicles. Kennywood followed suit three years later by installing its own version dubbed the Turnpike. It is believed Harton's friendship with Walt Disney, who at the time was a part owner of the company that manufactured the ride, was instrumental in helping West View Park land this new type of ride.

Soon, parks across the country were installing antique car rides. Another first for West View was a new two-story dark ride, built by Outdoor Dimensional Display Co., Inc., headed by creative genius Bill Tracy. Since West View Park had a strong partnership with the Allan Herschell Company, it supplied the ride vehicles and system. It was the only known collaboration between these companies to have ever occurred. The new Haunted House, with its fifteen displays and stunts, was an immediate success when it opened, bringing in 10,000 riders in its first three days of operation. Park renovations continued throughout the early part of the 1960s.

With the success of the Haunted House, Bill Tracy and Outdoor Dimensional Display Co., Inc. was brought in again to revitalize attractions. In 1964, extensive remodeling of Ride-N-Laff and the Mirror Maze occurred, with the new ride names now called Davey Jones Locker and Boot Hill, respectively. Previously in 1962, the Ride-N-Laff loading station and façade had been redesigned. The newly themed, and named, Davey Jones Locker featured five new tricks and a new front façade, featuring a replica of a sunken ship and the figure of a pirate. Costing $21,200, the ride became instantly popular when it opened during the early part of the school picnic days of the season.

Bill Tracy was known for his unique, colorful, and popular story-themed attractions. Many parks, such as Kennywood, Waldameer, Dorney Park, LeSourdsville Lake Park, Elitch Gardens, Hunt's Pier, Crescent Park, Idora Park, Lagoon, Lake Winnie, Trimpers, and Whalom Park, all had dark rides or walk-through attractions designed by Bill Tracy. Waldameer, Lagoon, and Lake Winnie still have these attractions in their parks. Since their debut, alterations have occurred, but the bulk of the attractions still stem from the creative mind of Bill Tracy. Themes for these attractions were jungles, pirates, haunted houses, medieval castles, mines, and the Old West, and in later years, there was a combination of themes. In a July 5, 1964, *Pittsburgh Press* newspaper article, the two new attractions were given much attention:

> "Boot Hill and Davey Jones Locker are still the biggest attractions at the park this year. The latter is an undersea voyage through the world of the 'Jolly Roger' while in Boot Hill, you walk through a series of dark corridors to visit scenes from the Old West."

Kennywood followed suit and opened the Ghost Ship in 1967. Both Davey Jones Locker and the Ghost Ship were popular attractions for their respective parks; some would say legendary and memorable.

Originally, Boot Hill was set up as a concession, with Tracy owning the attraction and receiving 35 percent of the income from the attraction over a three-year period. It was agreed that Tracy would erect all interior partitions, interior displays, the new prefabricated front, and wiring, at his expense. West View Park would have the option of purchasing all of the furnished material at 50 percent of the original cost. Due to what George Harton described as poor judgment by Tracy, Boot Hill missed its target opening date of May 15. Consequently, the new attraction did not open to the general public until June 24, 1964, costing both Tracy and West View a significant loss in school picnic revenue.

In June 1964, Tracy wrote to Harton and informed him he had overextended his operating capital and could no longer operate Boot Hill as a concession. Correspondence and price negotiations for the completed attraction ensued for the remainder of the year. On March 3, 1965, a buyout settlement was signed that left West View Park Company as the sole owner of Boot Hill.

Other 1964 improvements included new looks for the Penny Arcade and many of the game buildings, such as Fascination. Arrow Development, the same company that manufactured the Antique Cars, sold a new shooting gallery to West View and installed it in the building that formerly housed the Cuddle Up, at a cost of $11,237. Further remodeling came to the Auto Skooters in the form of a larger building and newer bumper cars. Modernization was key, and the newly enlarged building now featured thirty ride vehicles.

With more floor space, there was less bumping of the cars, which, in turn, reduced maintenance costs. The new Auto Scooter building and general ride improvements cost $49,695.

As management continued to add new features to cater to the many families who visited, a used Allan Herschell Company rodeo ride was purchased from Kennywood at a cost of $1,200, as well as a new Jolly Caterpillar, at a cost of $7,267. The Pony Barn, one of the oldest structures in the park, was renovated and remodeled in April. Know-

Park artist Jack Nofsigner

ing that the attraction was still popular with children, Harton saw the $4,820 investment as necessary. Disaster was avoided in Kiddieland when, on June 25, an overnight fire was spotted at the entrance to the Kiddie Dips. Repairs started quickly, and the ride reopened on Saturday, June 27.

Management also installed new and additional lightning fixtures at Danceland, while the Dips and Racing Whippet received new digital signs displaying safety messages to riders. Adding in the money spent on yearly painting, all of these investments totaled $103,988.00. The significant amount of money put back into the park showed the strong financial backing and performance of West View Park and the T.M. Harton Company. The year 1964 would prove to be the final year of major capital improvements and was very profitable. Each department was now up to the same expected standard when it came to setting operating budgets and projected income.

The year 1965 saw what would be the last major addition to West View Park: the Alpine Sky Ride. The ride featured gondolas hanging from a cable stretched over the midway. The gentle yet scenic ride provided riders with a unique view of the property unlike ever before. A similar ride had been installed at Elitch Gardens and would later appear at Cincinnati's Coney Island, Sandusky's Cedar Point, Disneyland, and at Erie's Waldameer Park. In addition to the Alpine Sky Ride, Harton also introduced the Trabant, a European ride that became one of the Chance Ride lineup of attractions.

Bill Cardille of Channel 11 and Janet Harton award a bike to a lucky winner on WIIC-NBC Family Day

West View continued to attract large crowds well into the 1960s by means of special events. Large crowds of all ages visited when WIIC broadcasted live wrestling matches from the Talkie Temple. WIIC personality Bill Cardille, better known as "Chilly" Billy from *Chiller Theatre*, was frequently scheduled to visit the park. He promoted various events and new rides, and, along with Harton, introduced WIIC Day in 1965. With the ever-growing popularity of Chiller Theater, Cardille even appeared with his monster friends at the Haunted House. Cardille was good friends with George Harton and, in 1965 with the help of WIIC's Chuck Moyer, created a promotional video for West View Park.

The constant improvements and additions to the park seemed never-ending, and the public was overjoyed each year when West View Park opened for the summer season. America was also changing culturally, by way of its clothing styles and music. The British Invasion of rock and pop music acts from the United Kingdom captured the eyes and ears of American teenagers, and the park was ready to embrace the new trends.

Rock 'n Roll Changes America

The British Invasion made its way to West View Park on Wednesday June 17, 1964. The Rolling Stones performed at Danceland the same night as Bobby Goldsboro, The Chiffons, Bobby Comstock, and The Pixies Three. The show was the seventh of a nine-city United States tour debut. Tickets were available for purchase at all National Record Marts for $1.50. The eleven-song set list performance by The Rolling Stones was the first of many concerts in Pittsburgh. While not as popular at the time in America as The Beatles, The Rolling Stones later became one of the most successful rock 'n roll bands in music history. They preceded The Beatles in performing in Pittsburgh by three months.

George Harton embraced the rock 'n roll generation and had groups perform at West View frequently. On August 21, 1963, The Beach Boys, then America's most popular band, performed at Danceland. Rock groups performed at either Danceland or the Talkie Temple. The Rolling Stones were booked solely because they were an inexpensive group. Harton had never heard of the group, which at the time was still known as The Rollin' Stones, not The Rolling Stones. As the park did for most of its radio advertising, radio spots

George Bodnar signed the $500 contract to have the Rolling Stones perform at Danceland

were played on KQV Radio. Tickets cost $1.50, but management became disappointed with ticket sales and began issuing free tickets to boost attendance numbers. By the following year, The Rolling Stones became internationally popular and too expensive for the park to book. Instead, the group returned in 1965 to play at the newly opened Civic Arena in downtown Pittsburgh. Another Decca Records group, Bill Haley and the Comets, also performed at Danceland. The June 8, 1955, performance featured the group at the height of their popularity, playing their hit song "Rock Around the Clock."

Most early amusement parks were either founded by or operated by railway companies. The country was home to numerous trolley parks, but gradually that era came to a close. Many of the parks founded by railway companies closed. Public transportation changed, and Pittsburghers wanting to take the No. 10 streetcar to West View Park were unable to after September 4, 1965. West View was one of the last major parks in the country to have its streetcar stop discontinued.

Change at the Helm

The success of West View Park seemed it would never end; however, behind the scenes, the future of the park was in question. After battling illness off and on for seven years, George M. Harton III was diagnosed with cancer in May 1965. After the cancer spread in January 1966, Harton lived only slightly longer and passed away on April 24, 1966. For the first time since his own father's passing in 1920, West View Park and T.M. Harton Company were left without a clear future and direction.

One reason the park survived without his leadership was the strong leadership team he inherited and developed. Throughout his tenure, Harton worked on creating a management team built on delegating responsibilities to other members of the management team. He even groomed both his daughter and son for responsibilities within the company and park; however, Harton's death created a family leadership crisis. George Bodnar determined the future was not bright for West View Park, and he left to become general manager of White Swan Amusement Park in nearby Moon Township. With Bodnar leaving, Jack Hickey was appointed general manager of West View Park. Prior to Bodnar's departure, Ed Vettel Jr. left in 1964 to become superintendent at Pontchartrain Beach Amusement Park, a position he held until the park closed in 1983. Replacing him as West View Park superintendent was his brother Robert, better known as Bud.

The golden years of West View Park appeared to be over. Many foresaw the end of the park's existence, but it continued to operate profitably after Harton's passing. In 1966, the park continued infrastructure improvements, relandscaping the main midway and completely renovating and enclosing the Games Mall, located next to the Flying Scooters. The radio tower was eventually dismantled, with the equipment moving to the park office. The building was repurposed for selling park novelty items.

In August, A.E. "Ed" Kountz assumed the role of president of the T.M. Harton Company. Kountz was the husband of Carice Kountz, mother of George Harton III, and majority shareholder. Due to the death of her son, Carice Kountz struggled to make decisions that were in the best interest for the park's future and family ownership. Additional family members who held ownership in West View Park Company were Charles Beares III, Janet Von Twistern, and Dr. George Harton IV. There was some hope Charles Beares III would return to West View Park; however, Carice Kountz was reluctant to relinquish control of major decision-making regarding the park's future. Knowing that correct decisions had to be made for West View to operate smoothly, the family put their trust in the hands of two faithful and trusted employees.

Alan Leanord, Jimmy Confer, Assistant Danceland manager, Janet Harton, G.M. Harton III, a park performer, and George Harton IV

Young riders prepare themselves for a ride on the Caterpillar

A group of employees at the prize redemption counter in the arcade

This bike ride was built in-house by the West View Park maintenance staff

The Helicopter ride was relocated from the main midway to Kiddieland, next to the Kiddie Dips in 1962. To the right of the Helicopters was the Kiddie Turtles, which was relocated to this spot from next to the Pony Track.

Huba Huba the Clown, George Harton IV, and Maria Heine

The Helicopter and Caterpillar ride, were both manufactured by the Allan Herschell Company. The Ferris Wheel was manufactured by the Eli-Bridge Company, the company who also manufactured the Krazy Daizy (Scrambler).

Ed Vettel Jr., inspecting the lift hill and chain on the Dips

Bob Vettel inspecting the Helicopter ride

John Hickey is pictured entertaining a group in the committee room

The Four Freshman performing at Danceland in 1961

Boru poses with guests during a Hot Dog Promotion Day

The Pony Ranch as seen in Kiddieland

Pat, Jo, Elaine working at the Pony Ranch

The street car is seen here at the West View Park stop, located next to the entrance of Danceland

The Free Act Stage was located next to administration building until 1961.

The Soda Bar, located directly across the midway from the administration building originally allowed guests to be able to walk into the building. By the 1960s, a counter was added to the middle section and guests could purchase drinks, sandwiches, french fries, corn dogs, pizza, and soft drinks.

The Pony Cart ride was added to
Kiddieland in 1941

The Scooters sat across the midway from
the Whip

The Ferris Wheel was a popular ride that offered great views of the park and the valley

By the late 1950s, the park began to install additional rides on the midway including an Allan Herschell Looper. As more rides were installed on the main midway, trees which once provided shade were removed.

Ride Operators at work on the Ferris Wheel. Operators had to balance the ride in patterns so that rider weight was distributed evenly amongst all ride vehicles. Once the ride was loaded, the ride cycle would begin.

The Mirror Maze featured a monkey band at its entrance. A red line was painted on the floor showing the way to exit, to help avoid injuries.

The Rock-O-Plane was manufactured by Eyerly Aircraft

The Flying Scooter, manufactured by Bisch-Rocco, was an interactive flying ride with a stationary rear wing and a moveable front wing that allowed guests to control the flight of their vehicle as the ride rotated.

The Kiddie Whip was a popular kiddie attraction as was its popular larger counterpart located next to the Dips.

The Up-C-Dazy (Flying Cages) was a short-lived attraction at the park and sat on the spot previously occupied by the Loop-o-Plane, Moon Rocket, Rotor, and Round Up. The Round Up was re-introduced and replaced the Up-C-Dazy for the 1967 season.

Summer drivers on Route 19, frequently waited at the traffic light and saw this view of the Dips train roaring around its famous turnaround

Davey Jones Locker was introduced in 1964 and featured five new tricks. Riders entered the attraction through a whale's mouth and then encountered themselves below a lake with someone fishing. Each scene lasted roughly 6 seconds.

The Krazy Dazy Orbit was brought in to replace the spot formerly occupied by the Free Act Stage.

West View Park featured a lot of art-deco architecture with neon lighting. To the left is the Haunted Swing attraction, which was located next to the Mirror Maze

Aerial view of West View Park as seen in the late 1950s

Jack at
the Helm

West View Park operations were now in the hands of trusted and
newly appointed General Manager John "Jack" Hickey Jr. and Executive Secretary Margaret Habel. Hickey was a likeable and highly respected individual
within the amusement industry who started working at West View Park with
his father, John Sr., in 1948. Like his father, Jack Hickey's background was in
the picnic and group sales business. Ron Beck, who worked with Habel and
Hickey, said:

> "It was my understanding that Mrs. Habel and Mr. Hickey managed the op-
> erations of the park. I believe the two had a very good working relationship.
> Both Mr. Hickey and Mrs. Habel were very pleasant and friendly. Mrs. Habel
> always maintained a very polite, very professional appearance, as if she was
> sitting in a board room meeting. She was always neatly dressed in business
> attire and her appearance and demeanor always commanded respect."

The new 1967 season saw the return of a popular ride, the Round Up. While
the late 1960s were a successful time for many amusement parks, some parks,
such as Riverview Park outside Chicago, and Euclid Beach Park, outside

General Manager Jack Hickey (left) stands next to employee Jim "Cuddles" Kuhn

Cleveland, closed forever. Tensions were growing in America, too, as the country found itself fighting in the Vietnam War, the fallout of which was non-support of our service men and women, which was frowned upon. Racial tensions also heightened throughout the country.

Park attendance increased during these years since Pittsburghers were traveling less. With the gasoline shortage of the late 1960s, parks such as West View and Kennywood experienced strong attendance and revenue. West View Park had some of its strongest years in the late 1960s, largely due to the purchases of new attractions in the first half of the decade. West View Park featured a great lineup of attractive rides catering to families, all of which were situated between the park's star attractions, the Dips and Racing Whippet. Despite steel coasters being introduced, wooden roller coasters saw a revival and West View's excellent and unique wooden roller coasters helped keep the park relevant.

The Late 1960s

Starting in the 1960s, amusement parks began to diversify and create an atmosphere that wasn't universal from park to park. Rides from Europe became stars, as did custom-designed steel roller coasters. Parks no longer featured the same ride lineup. The possibility of West View Park adding an Arrow Development log flume ride or custom steel coaster that sent riders upside down was certainly a possibility. In 1966, there were only five log flumes in operation in the United States. By the time Kennywood installed a flume ride called the Log Jammer in 1975, that number had greatly increased. Jack Hickey and Margaret Habel certainly wanted to maintain the standards set by George Harton. The park had one of the first Arrow Development antique car rides and one of the first Trabant rides imported from Europe.

Prior to the passing of George Harton, multiple plans had been under consideration for new rides and park projects. George Bodnar, the assistant general manager, began working closely with Harton to analyze and develop a long-term plan for the park. In the early 1960s, a plan was laid out to establish a pay one price admission system and eliminate the use of individual ride and refreshment tickets. For years, the amusement industry was strictly a cash transaction business; everything was purchased and/or sold using cash. With no system to track theft, as most businesses have today, businesses operated under the mindset of honesty. Theft occurred regularly and payment did not always occur for food or ride admission. Employees even pocketed tickets and money handed to them.

Knowing that theft was an issue, Harton hired a private undercover investigator to observe employees regularly. Unbeknownst to anyone else, the undercover investigator took his young daughter to the park in order to fit in as a regular guest. When hard evidence was presented to George Harton by the investigator, he knew he had to implement a pay one price admission system. Harton planned to turn West View Park into a gated park with controlled access, but the plan was never implemented.

Although Harton's death halted some plans, others in middle management decided to step up. Tom "Skip" Morrow took on the role of operations manager. He was also instrumental in hiring the seasonal workers before and during each season. The park hired mostly area high school students from North Hills, North Allegheny, or other nearby schools. Most college students who worked at the park grew up patronizing the park. In addition, the park hired retired individuals. Interviews typically lasted about ten minutes and took place over several days. For the employees who drove a car to work, any front-line employee or manager had a private parking lot that sat directly behind the carousel. Starting at West View as a seasonal employee in the late 1950s, Skip Morrow was a graduate of California University of Pennsylvania. Had he not had an active interest in the amusement business; he probably would've been a teacher, as he was an education major. His personality

Tom "Skip" Morrow, Assistant General Manager and Operations Manager

and education are what made Morrow a great leader and manager. Those who worked for Morrow saw him as a genuine mentor and encouraging boss. Former employee Al Snyder said:

> "Skip Morrow was a fun guy to work for. He loved his audio and did the audio for Danceland. Skip always had a smile on his face."

While Hickey had an office in the administration building, Morrow maintained offices at both Danceland and in the back of the arcade. Each morning, Skip Morrow's voice, dubbed the Voice of West View Park, played over the public address system:

> "Good Morning, and Welcome to West View Park. The time is now 11 a.m., and West View Park is now open!"

Following the announcement was the playing of the song "St. Louis Blues." When the park closed, Morrow played "Goodnight, Sweetheart, Goodnight," by The Spaniels. Former West View Park employee Tom Benson, who worked directly with Skip Morrow, said Morrow was always developing or implementing something new:

> "He was starting a new teen club in Danceland and wanted a group of advisors from local high schools. We were able to get involved with that and spent a couple of months recruiting others to the group from North Hills High and North Allegheny High. We even went on a local dance show on WIIC TV to promote the place. In early December 1967, the PRISM opened."

Morrow envisioned the PRISM to be similar to the Whiskey a Go Go in California. The PRISM existed to capture the young teenage youth rock movement and was later transformed into a psychedelic color and light show. Overhead projectors and posters were brought in, as were avant-garde bands. Skip Morrow tried to tap into different interests of the high school consultants who worked both on and during the PRISM shows. As the teenage culture was changing, so were people's attitudes and respect for one another. The crowds that came on Saturdays started to visit on Friday nights. Unfortunately, for the West View Park Police Department, fights occurred regularly.

Saturday nights at Danceland were extremely popular, with local DJ Mad Mike Metrovich, from 1640AM WZUM, playing his own brand of oldies he dubbed Mad Mike Moldies. The crowd consisted of locals and primarily

Tom Benson seen in the parking lot with a coworker

young folks from the North Side. These year-round dances ran smoothly and on their own, as did the Sunday night Old People's Dances. The crowds for the old-time big band and swing dancing held steady until Danceland's last days. When the PRISM closed, Danceland had been only operating on a limited schedule, open one or two days a week. As the 1968 summer season approached, the PRISM became a memory and the employees began preparing for another operating season.

The park continued to thrive under General Manager Jack Hickey due to strong middle-management. Jim Duncan managed the games department, and the West View Refreshment Company was run by a number of managers, including Harry Habel and Bob Wadsworth. Harry Habel, whose wife was Margaret Habel, had worked in multiple roles since joining the management team in 1948. Habel, head of West View Refreshment Company, was also involved in non-concession park operations. He helped manage Danceland and worked with Jack Hickey to sell school picnic tickets and book company and

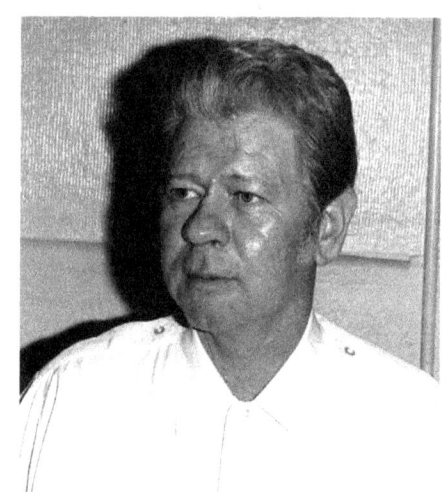

Jim "The Chief" Miller

group picnics. The park also employed several police officers, led by Chief Jim Miller—the Chief.—whose office was inside the park's administration building. The borough of West View deputized West View Park police officers, complete with real badges, training, and a licensee to carry a concealed weapon. Park officers were stationed throughout the park's midways and parking lots. The staff took safety and security seriously and didn't hesitate in removing individuals looking to cause issues.

"I worked at the hat stand during the summers of 1968 and 1969. My boss was Jim Duncan and his assistant was Wayne Sarver. I loved my job and was never bored. Once a year, Jim would take the games mall employees to Brady's Bend on his boat. I have so many memories of West View Park school picnics with my cousin Sam and then as an employee. It was a magical place!"

Mary Ann Walter – Pittsburgh, PA

Guests obtaining hats during a picnic giveaway

Beginning in the late 1960s, the Park was the host site of the Tea Tournament, which was a battle of the bands contest between bands from Western Pennsylvania. The event went on all summer long on the Showtime stage, formally known as the Talkie Temple. Big named groups such as Tommy James and the Shondells even performed during these shows. Winners of the local Tea Tournament went on to the national show held in Lambert, New Jersey, to compete for a recording deal. The modern-day versions of this early concept are *American Idol* and *The Voice*. The Tea Tournament was Jack Hickey and Margaret Habel's immediate plan to continue the George Harton way of innovative and creative marketing.

In addition to adapting to new forms of entertainment, Hickey introduced new rides every year, from 1969–1972. These rides included a new C.P. Huntingdon train, a hydraulic Paratrooper, and Tempest. In addition, the double Ferris wheel, or sky wheel, was a leased ride on a traveling circuit that made an appearance in 1969 and 1970. The tall erector set-like structure stood and rotated at heights of 127 feet.

Pete's Pipers play at the PRISM on opening night

The 1970s – A New Decade

In the 1970s, Hickey attempted to attract outside vendors to West View for marketing and promotional purposes. The goal behind the idea was to develop a new marketing strategy while giving back to the community. Religious organizations were invited to rent the park to film short movies. Lutheran Ministries answered the call and hired George Romero to develop a film about aging Americans over a two-day period. The film, titled *The Amusement Park*, went unreleased until the film was rediscovered and restored for public showing in 2019.

"The Amusement Park" in production at West View Park

By the 1970s, CB (citizen band) radios were becoming common, and amusement parks began utilizing radios to communicate with staff. West View implemented the use of radios throughout the park. Originally used for the parking lot staff, they were quickly adopted for use by park security officers and other departments. The three parking lots on the property were organized and numbered. Parking lot 1 was located on the hill next to Danceland; parking lot 2 was located at the main entrance (closest to Route 19); and parking lot 2A was located on the hill next to the Dips.

A serious 1971 fatal accident occurred on the Dips when a rider was thrown out of the train's last seat and dragged along the tracks. Earlier that same season, a rider had fallen off the Racing Whippet. The rider on the Dips came directly from the Bavarian Room onto the ride and stood at some point during the ride. The trains consisted of industry standard stationary lap bars and a leather strap, something that was common in the industry.

Today, almost every roller coaster train has either single seat or individual lap bars with individual seat belts. This design strongly helps prevent accidents from occurring. The Dips was closed so the trains could be modified. Management purchased locking lap bars and mechanisms from the National Amusement Device Company (NAD), which had provided parts for the coaster trains since their inception. The trains, although designed and built by Ed Vettel, were very similar to the roller coaster trains designed and built by NAD. Vettel simply improved upon the design to maneuver the track better and create less stress on the ride.

In 1972, a PA system was added to the C.P. Huntington train that had replaced the NAD miniature railroad train. Morrow was looking for new ways to update the ride, and an idea he had was sparked by a brochure he had on the history of Collis Potter Huntington. A script by employees Tom Benson and Jim Kuhns was then developed and written about the history of the train and utilized on the ride for passengers to listen to while riding. New sound effects and ride audio tracks were added to the Haunted House. Morrow and his assistant, Tom Kissel, provided the voices. Rock music was later added to a newer ride on the midway, The Tempest. Helping in this process was Tom Benson, who helped create slideshow presentations for employee orientation and training. Helping with the voice work was another employee, Peggy Lindow. Both employees did all of the photography, writing, and editing for the orientation slide show. All of this work was completed using equipment located in Danceland. Most likely ahead of its time, this new orientation training lasted only one season, as did the Sweeperette crew. The idea stemmed from a Cedar Point concept of a crew of workers walking around the park with brooms and dustpans to maintain West View's cleanliness and image. Many of these ideas were developed from operational practices used at Disney World and Cedar Point. Park benches were also repainted, moving from a dark green color to a light green or yellow.

Loss of a Park Landmark

Tragedy struck the park on the night of Saturday, September 29, 1973. Danceland was destroyed when a spark occurred on the neon sign located at the building's main entrance. The building was a complete loss and suffered $1 million in damages. On Friday, the day before the fire, J.R. Henry was preparing Danceland for a Fraternal Order of Police private party event. He recalled:

> "Hickey came by Danceland that day to mention that the "a" in the neon Danceland sign above the entrance was burned out and that he wanted a call to be put in on Monday so the sign could get fixed."

Jim Miller Jr., whose father, Jim Miller Sr., was chief of police at West View Park, also worked at West View Park from 1970–1977 and for a time after the park closed. Jim Jr. was inside Danceland working when the front door ticket taker (a female employee) came inside and said she smelled smoke. J.R. Henry, Tom Benson, and other employees then noticed the doorbell had shorted out and they smelled smoke toward the front door. They then decided to have someone take a look in the ceiling. Miller climbed up into the ceiling and informed the others the ceiling was on fire and the fire was spreading. Benson said:

> "We noticed it immediately and began clearing the house. Ken Furrer (another worker that night) and I were the last two out. He took one side and I the other, as we ran to the back of the building and crossed and ran back to the front. We wanted to make sure we got everyone out. By that time, flames were coming out of the ceiling."

As fire departments set up to battle the blaze, park management and employees watched the events unfold from the miniature golf building across from Danceland. After the fire, Carice Kountz sought to sell the park. The ownership group of Kennywood expressed interest, however Kountz couldn't see the park being owned by anyone outside the Harton Family.

Luckily, all 540 individuals attending and working the event were safely evacuated through the building's five exits. When the fire was spotted, Tommy Payne and his band from Bridgeville were playing the 1940s Harry James hit "You Made Me Love You." It was a sad yet meaningful song to end the story of Danceland. Unfortunately, the building burned to the ground.

When Park Superintendent Bob Vettel received a phone call that night about the fire, Vettel feared his office would be lost in the blaze due to the direction of the wind and intense heat. Bud's wife and daughter Kathy cleared the maintenance office of important documents. Vettel's office inside the maintenance and sign shop was located behind the cafeteria, directly below the hill where Danceland was located. Thankfully, the maintenance offices and park sign shop were spared.

Most of the concrete block around the outside of the building survived the fire, but the rest of the building constructed of wood was gutted by flames. Pittsburgh lost an iconic entertainment venue, and West View Park lost its heart. While the carousel, legendary roller coasters, and midway were the soul of the park, Danceland brought out the best in couples and was a hot spot for creating the magic that enabled people to fall in love.

Numerous fire departments were called in and battled the blaze for twelve hours. By the next morning, the smell of burning wood filled the park and West View Borough. The loss of the iconic building was an emotional roller coaster ride for ownership and management. For months, the structure sat while the insurance company settled the claim. Jack Hickey estimated reconstruction would cost a half million dollars. While numbers had fallen from what used to be 1,000 guests a night to only 300, Hickey was in favor of replacing Danceland.

West View Park moved forward as a summer operation rather than a year-round operation. After the fire, majority stockholder Carice Kountz decided not to rebuild Danceland, and the remaining parts of the building were demolished. To many people's dismay, the building was not rebuilt or land repurposed. Personal memories for Pittsburghers, employees, and owners came rushing back once it was known the building was a complete loss. The area that was once occupied by Danceland was leveled and grass planted. Upon hearing about the fire, Janet Von Twistern booked a flight to Pittsburgh and said:

> "The fire smoldered for three days. A line of cars slowly drove by for days. It was like a funeral procession."

Her brother, Dr. George Harton IV, said:

> "Danceland had been the shining star for year-round revenue."

The hill where Danceland stood never looked the same. The lone survivor from the fire was the American Bald Eagle that sat on top of the flagpole outside the building. As a way to remember the building and memories, Bob Vettel took the eagle and later gave it to his daughter Kathy for a keepsake.

Danceland's flagpole eagle

West View Park without Danceland

After the fire, Habel and Hickey continued to budget for capital improvements, including infrastructure and roller coaster maintenance. Although the fire was a setback, 1974 and 1975 were successful years financially, in spite of declining attendance. Jack Nofsinger returned to the park after the 1974 season to restore the entire carousel for the 1975 season. The ride's frame, panels, and horses were repainted, and Nofsinger painted the center panels of the ride in 1948. He also removed each figure from the ride so that he could properly paint them and make any necessary repairs. This was the second time he had completely restored the carousel. Because the project was a major undertaking, Jack had his then 21-year-old son Jack help. Although the carousel was restored, Carice and A.E. Kountz continued to limit the expenditures of improvements. Jack Hickey, Margaret Habel, and Tom Morrow thought otherwise, and believed West View was still worthy of a major capital project. The three minority stockholders—Charles Beares III, Janet Von Twistern, and Dr. George Harton IV—did not even have a vote or voice in the matter. With Danceland gone, teenagers and workers alike made time to congregate in the Game Mall and Arcade. Former employee Scott Kerr remembered:

> "There were between 50–70 pinball machines inside the arcade. The pinball machines ran on the outside of the arcade and middle row. Other machines were dated by the 1970s. There were 1940s' machines with postcards, sport stars, and Hollywood stars. The first computerized games were purchased in the mid-1970s, 1973, or 1974. It was called Computer Space. It was a single player game, cost 25 cents, black and white, made by Nutting Company. Skee-Ball was next to Davey Jones Locker, not in the arcade. The arcade had a jukebox inside and spin-art booth. There was also a hockey puck bowler game. Employees would gather after park hours at the jukebox. Our group would hang out and have a dance social."

When Cedar Point introduced the new Arrow Development Corkscrew in 1976, Jack Hickey and Skip Morrow were so impressed with the ride design that they took multiple trips to Cedar Point to ride and learn about the new sensation. The two of them decided West View Park needed a new roller coaster, and the Corkscrew would be the next new major ride installation. Plans called for the ride to be installed in the area near the Antique Cars. While the ideas were extremely exciting, the Corkscrew never made an appearance at West View. Ron Beck, who worked as an accountant at the park and reported directly to Habel, explained what he remembered about the situation:

> "I remember having some chats with Mr. Hickey. He told me that the park had its origins in West View because it was the outer loop of the streetcar line. He lamented that the park was limited in terms of expansion because of real estate. Additionally, a lot of people were starting to drive or fly to Orlando's Magic Kingdom. It became obvious to me that Mrs. Habel and Mr. Hickey saw the handwriting on the wall. West View Park was limited in what it could do. Mrs. Habel and Mr. Hickey had the vision and they could see the competition. They basically maintained and marginally improved the status quo. I give them a lot of credit for that and deep down shared their sense of pain and loss when the park closed."

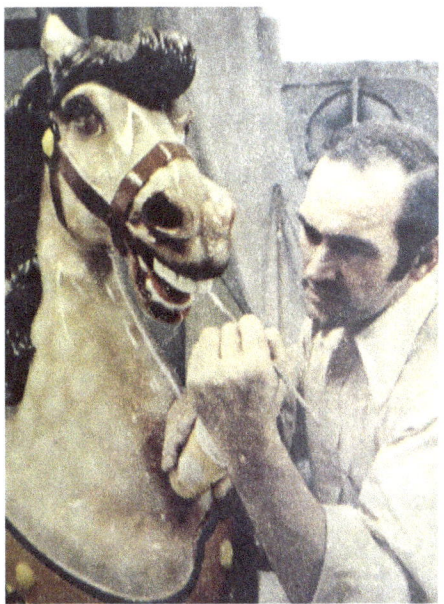

Jack Nofsinger was brought back to the park to repaint and refurbish the Carousel during the 1974/1975 offseason

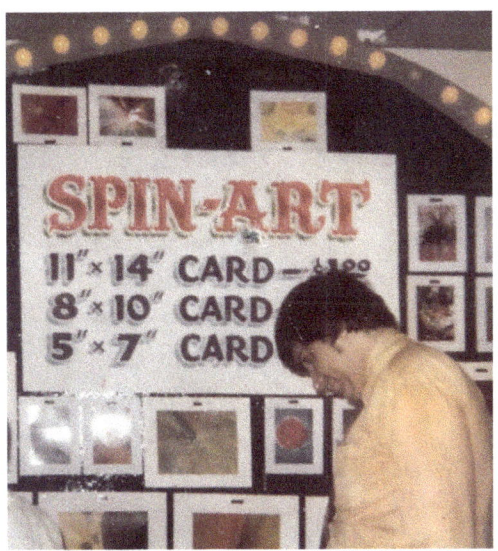

Upon entering the arcade, guests were greeted by the photo booth. To the far left corner was the jukebox. The most popular pinball machines was "Ten Spot." Claw machines could be found at the Games Mall. To the right of the arcade was Tom Morrows office. During the winter, it was the security office and maintenance winter repair shop for the games.

West View Park never adopted an official uniform for seasonal employees but had employees wear jeans and nice casual clothing.

Ice Balls were a popular summer park treat. The hanging sign was hand painted, similar to most signage in the park.

Scott Kerr at work in the parking lot

To manage payroll in a more efficient manner, West View operated with a skeleton crew on some days. This was done, primarily, because ride operators and games attendants manned multiple rides or games. In the early 1970s, picnics began moving to Kennywood. Other parks throughout the industry experienced the same issues. Many of those parks had already closed or were on the brink of closure, and the amusement park business was changing. New operators and new ideas were in and the old style of business was out and considered old-fashioned. West View Park was landlocked, and expansion was tough due to the local neighborhood and government.

Meanwhile, Kennywood, which debuted the Thunderbolt in 1968, had established itself as a roller coaster park, something Kennywood ownership never truly embraced. Prior to the Thunderbolt, Kennywood's roller coasters were not recognized within the industry or in the Pittsburgh market as great rides. The Thunderbolt, designed by Andy Vettel, with consulting from John Allen of the Philadelphia Toboggan Company, gave Kennywood instant recognition and helped spark a revival of interest in wooden roller coasters. In a 1974 *New York Times* article, Kennywood's Thunderbolt was named the "Ultimate Roller Coaster." Not pleased with the article, Jack Hickey and other members of West View Park's staff attempted to contact the *New York Times* on multiple occasions regarding the article.

Hickey wasn't necessarily upset at the list, but he certainly believed West View's roller coasters were superior to Kennywood's. In particular, he believed West View's coaster, specifically the Dips, was the greatest coaster never discovered. The Kennywood management team was equally surprised when they learned the Thunderbolt was named number one. Members of Kennywood management were surprised that West View's roller coasters were not listed, as they were indeed superior to Kennywood's.

Jean Burns MacDonald, who started working as a ride operator on the Flying Scooter and Whip in 1974, began working on the Dips one month into the 1975 season. Jean became the first female to work on the

Jack Hickey

Employee credentials and badges from the 1970s

ride. In the late 1970s, there was a crew of six that operated the ride, led by Vince Vulik, who also helped maintain the ride and performed maintenance on the ride prior to opening. The Dips had a total of four trains. After the park made an operational change to only operate with two trains, one train was used for parts while a third train sat on the transfer track and was used on a rotating schedule with the other two operating trains. The operators relied on the relay board to light up and the bell to sound when the train in the station needed to be dispatched. The patrons sitting in the train at the loading station were dispatched for their ride at the sound of the bell, meaning one train had gone around the bend by Route 19. Burns MacDonald recalled:

> "I remember it was a good mix of older retired and younger people working. People came off the rides happy. I remember Mr. Hickey working at the park. He was always picking up garbage. He loved the park."

Rich Wahlster, who operated the Racing Whippet during the West View's final two seasons, remembered that the coasters were some of the finest ever designed. He explained that management was dealt a tough hand, due to a variety of reasons, but when it came to the rides, he said:

> "Bob Vettel, aka "Buddy," did a great job keeping things running."

Regardless of what was occurring with the owners, the park continued to be well operated. One of the noticeable changes to the rides was the repainting of the trains on the Dips and Racing Whippet in 1976. To recognize the 100th anniversary of the United States, the roller coaster trains were painted red, white, and blue. They remained those colors for West View's final season in 1977.

The Racing Whippet remained widely popular into the 1970s. Riders had to be 52" to ride alone on both the Racing Whippet and Dips.

The West View Park marquee sign could be found along Route 19.

Maintenance Employees, Al Francischiani and Cart Miller

Margaret Habel working at her desk which was located at the top of the steps leading to the second floor of the administration building

A young guest feeds Porky the Paper Eater. These popular trash eaters were designed and sold by the Batt Family of Ponchartrain Beach.

Kathy Vettel takes a break from her shift to take a photo at the parking lot that was named after her by co-worker Tom Benson.

The Racing Whippet originally had catwalks along the track. When the catwalks were removed, the maintenance employees would walk on the track ties during daily inspections

When the last remaining section of the lake was filled in for the 1977 season, the 1937 fountain was removed and the miniature train route was altered to complete a loop around the Dips instead of the lake. When Bob Vettel or anyone in the Vettel Family talked about his father or their history in roller coaster construction/design, the Dips was always the first roller coaster to come up.

The Dips travels around its famous turnaround located next to Route 19

West View Park was still attracting large crowds well into the 1970s

While tastes in music changed, the Talkie Temple remained a popular spot to host free concerts and entertainment. In the 1970s, it was common for rock and roll groups to perform on the Talkie Temple stage

Tom "Skip" Morrow is pictured here sitting on the Danceland crystal ball after it was pulled from the fire. The park restored and sold the crystal ball.

The fountain was added in 1937 and was removed after the 1976 season when the last section of the lake was filled in.

Boot Hill was a popular walk-thru attraction at the park from 1964-1977. The attraction replaced both the Mirror Maze and Haunted Swing. Boot Hill featured Bill Tracy's Old Mill Scene, a Jail Cell Maze, a Western Bar scene, and a final scene of hands in a toilet.

By 1977, the Bug had already started to become a rare ride to find at amusement parks. Kennywood's Turtle is the last remaining ride of its kind still in operation

When the Haunted House opened, it featured an outdoor second story section of track without a roof. A roof was added shortly after the ride was added to avoid issues with rain water. The two-story dark ride featured rocking skeletons, black lights, a spinning tunnel, falling barrels, a grave robber scene, and a flying witch.

Chapter 8

The Final Season

Rumors of the park becoming a unionized workforce were said to have taken place; however, the park staff never unionized. Carice Kountz, the majority owner, turned 92 in January and was homebound since 1966. Her husband, and attorney, A.E. Kountz, was also elderly, homebound, and bedridden. In his earlier years, Kountz specialized in bankruptcy law and headed a prominent law firm in Pittsburgh. Upon marrying into the Harton Family, Kountz studied the amusement industry and saw a trend that family-owned parks would continue to close or be sold to corporations. Jack Hickey and Margaret Habel knew the end had arrived.

By 1977, West View Park was one of the few remaining large sized family-owned parks still afloat in what was starting to become an industry dominated by theme parks and high insurance costs. High insurance costs continued to hinder family-owned parks, while the major theme parks owned by corporations were able to continue without concern. School district consolidation impacted both West View Park and Kennywood. The trend of family-owned parks closing or selling to larger companies was a trend that continued throughout the 1980s. By the end of the 1980s, most of

Looking from the entrance to Kiddieland, guests saw the Racing Whippet station and Boot Hill in the distance.

Andy Vettel (standing next to the Whip car), ran a highly successful maintenance department with Fred Weber at Kennywood

the country's family-owned amusement parks were all but a memory. When West View Park closed in 1977, there were roughly only 30 amusement parks left in Pennsylvania.

More Pennsylvania parks closed in the following years: Cascade Park & Hanson's Amusement Park in 1984, Rocky Glen Park and Lakeview Park in 1987, Angela Park in 1988, White Swan Park in 1990, and Williams Grove Park in 2005. By 2020, the number of parks in the Commonwealth of Pennsylvania declined to fourteen. At one time, Pennsylvania was flooded with amusement parks and the most roller coaster track in the world. This was due to Pittsburgh's unique role in growing the amusement industry along with the ride manufacturers and distributers headquartered in Pennsylvania. While a lot of Pennsylvania parks have closed, those that remain in operation are some of the oldest continuing operating parks in the country.

Janet Von Twistern and her brother, Dr. George Harton IV, knew 1977 was going to be the last operating season. Wanting their own children to experience the park, both Janet and George visited multiple times in 1977 with their children. In its final year of operation, West View Park opened only eighty days and hosted twenty school picnics. In prior seasons, the park had hosted as many as forty-five school districts for a day of summer fun. Jack Hickey did not shy away from rumors claiming West View struggled since 1966 or since 1973. Despite the rumors, West View remained profitable each season. The park's final season was plagued by low attendance and minor maintenance-related issues. And, as the operating days went by, the midways no longer bustled with patrons.

Kennywood's Survival

Throughout the years, West View and Kennywood maintained a strong friendly relationship and frequently communicated with each other. Andy Quinn, whose family, along with the Henningers, owned and operated crosstown competitor Kennywood, said they (Kennywood ownership and management) talked with, and saw, Jack Hickey often:

> "I remember when West View was still open, Jack (Hickey) used to stop at Kennywood on Labor Day because he lived in McKeesport. He had to travel

past Kennywood every day to and from his job at West View. And, he was good friends with Carl Henninger and Carl Hughes. He and I subsequently became good friends also. We knew West View was performing well because Jack would tell us."

When discussing the gentleman's agreement of group picnics at West View and Kennywood, Andy said:

"We had an agreement with West View. We would not steal any of West View's picnics they had in those days, Mellon Bank and the Carpenters Union. The deal was, we wouldn't go after a West View Picnic and they wouldn't go after a Kennywood picnic. When West View closed, then all of a sudden, those picnics became ours. School picnics through the 1970s represented almost 65–70 percent of our business. But, slowly, that started to change as the schools changed. On the other hand, industrial picnics and other types of picnics grew exponentially."

Kennywood's location was key to obtaining industrial picnics, unlike West View Park. West View, on the other hand, was a bit more difficult to travel to because it was within the town of West View and off the main highways. Kennywood's location in the Steel Valley, where the steel and railroad industries were primarily located, proved vital to Kennywood's survival. Large companies such as Westinghouse Electric and United States Steel held their company picnics at Kennywood every summer. While Kennywood hosted Westinghouse and United States Steel, West View hosted Mellon Bank and H.J. Heinz.

For the 1977 season, Davey Jones Locker was re-themed as Land of Giants. At the same time, prices for new equipment and maintenance costs continued to rise. Thanks to Bob "Bud" Vettel and the entire maintenance team, the Dips and Racing Whippet remained in top operating condition. If there is one thing Pittsburghers know about wooden roller coasters, it's that they are well maintained. Wooden roller coaster maintenance at West View and Kennywood can be attributed to the Vettel family and their vast knowledge of roller coaster designs and engineering. Every member of the Vettel family active in the industry shared their knowledge and expertise on wooden coaster maintenance and passed it on to the next generation. And according to industry experts, Kennywood's wooden roller coasters are some of the best maintained wooden roller coasters in the country, proving that they continue to maintain the legacy and standards established by the Vettels. At both West View and Kennywood, the Vettels emphasized the importance of high-quality, on-going maintenance.

Bob "Bud" Vettel, West View Park Maintenance Superintendent

When West View Park prepared to open for the 1977 season, management encountered issues in June when attendance numbers did not meet expectations. Hickey and Habel were forced to scale back to a limited operating schedule. As Jack Hickey explained to the *Pittsburgh Press*, from July until Labor Day, the Park would operate on an on-again, off-again basis. Jack Hickey said school closings and mergers hurt the park's main source of revenue:

> "This was a picnic park, not a transient park. We had to have an event scheduled here or there wouldn't be anyone who showed up. Now the districts are bigger, but we only get one shot at a group of people, instead of two or three," said Hickey. "It's not the park, it's the people that have changed."

Hickey, who was by now a 29-year veteran of the amusement industry, knew the older traditional family-orientated parks could not resist change. The annual increase of insurance did not help and neither did the park being situated in a neighborhood that didn't allow for expansion. Hickey said:

> "There just aren't many people left in the amusement park business anymore, and pretty soon there won't be any parks like this one."

People began speculating that the growth of major theme parks major theme parks especially those in just a few hours away from Pittsburgh such as Cedar Point, Geauga Lake and Sea World Ohio drew guests away from West View Park. Hickey disagreed:

> "But I don't think they affected us here too much. Those are transient parks, vacation spots where people might stop once."

The Round Up was manufactured by Frank Hrubetz & Company.

Following the completion of each operating season, West View Park employees would gather one last time for a small picnic the Saturday after Labor Day in Kiddieland. Then in the days following, the ride maintenance crew started their winterization projects. The rides became skeletons of what guests saw during the summer, leaving only ride platforms and frames. Ride vehicles, sweeps, lights, and various parts found a winter home in the Games Mall, Carousel building and/or maintenance shops. However, the days following Labor Day 1977, were much different than previous years.

> "The last day the park was open in 1977, our crew (Racing Whippet) was getting ready to close the Whippet for the night. I said 'why don't we all go for a last ride.' We were able to lock the back brakes so the trains would stop by themselves. The whole crew except for me jumped in the trains. I sent both trains out and jumped in one as it was going up the lift hill. There was no who was operating the ride right now. It was so odd seeing the whole crew in the trains and no one in the station. Funny thing was when I said go for one last ride, none of us knew that would be the final ride forever."
>
> *Rich Walhster – Pittsburgh, PA*

Various ticket books and tickets from West View's last operating season

West View Park Closes Forever

Jack Hickey grew up in the amusement business, having joined his father at West View Park upon graduating from Duquesne University in 1948. The thought of selling off the park's equipment was quite difficult for Hickey and members of the Harton family. Both Hickey and Margaret Habel had seen West View Park at its best and worst times, but Hickey probably didn't expect he would be the last employee of the once powerful T.M. Harton Company. In a surprising move, an anonymous letter signed by West View Park employees, was sent to Janet Von Twistern, asking her to "Save The Park." It was clear the employees, regardless of their employment status, loved the park. To this day, it is unknown who sent the letter, but Janet believes Margaret Habel sent the letter in a last-ditch effort to keep West View Park open.

When the staff was informed West View Park would close, they were shocked. Rumors had circulated for years, and even as the 1977 season began, park employees assumed West View would remain open because Davey Jones Locker was re-themed into Land of Giants. Although the 1977 season was a difficult operating season, the park maintained its safety record until the final operating day. At the conclusion of the 1977 season, locals noticed the "See You Next Year" sign was missing from the sign by Route 19. West View Park had completed its seventy-first and final season. Jack Hickey and Margaret Habel continued to report to work at the one-time bustling amusement park, sitting in the same administration building where members of the Beares and Harton families had worked. Now Hickey and Habel were tasked with selling all of the park's movable assets.

In fall 1976, Assistant Manager Tom "Skip" Morrow secured a new position as operations manager at Canobie Lake Park in New Hampshire. Morrow would go on to make a name for himself by impacting the lives of many employees at Canobie Lake Park, some of whom went on to have successful careers in the amusement industry. Morrow's leadership helped push Canobie Lake Park and parks of the New England Association of Amusement Parks and Attractions (NEAAPA) forward in the next decades. Eventually named president of the association, and affectionately known as Mr. NEAAPA for his years of dedication, the organization hosts the annual Tom Morrow Dinner and IAAPA Social during the week of the annual IAAPA Attractions Expo.

The Haunted House was mostly repurposed into the Fright Zone at Erieview Park

The Racing Whippet was cleverly designed to take advantage of the valley. It was the only Racing Coaster designed by Ed Vettel.

One of Morrow's last assistants at West View Park was Tom Moulton. Moulton, who attended college while working at West View Park, had aspirations of making a career in the amusement industry. Moulton achieved that goal when he went to work for LeSourdsville Park, Geauga Lake, and the Six Flags theme park chain.

As the days passed, rides began to disappear from the once popular Pittsburgh amusement park. In an age when park auctions and coaster preservation were in its infancy, West View Park slowly became a memory. Many of the rides were sold to now closed parks such as Cascade Park in New Castle, Magic Valley located in the Poconos, and even Massachusetts Whalom Park. Knoebels Amusement Resort, located in Elysburg, Pennsylvania, purchased equipment from West View Park. The unique double-decker Haunted House dark ride was eventually broken up, with most of it being sold to what became known as Erieview Park in Geneva, Ohio. The ride survived as a one-story ride, retaining some of the scenes and ride system. Known as The Fright Zone, the attraction closed after the 2006 season, when Erieview Park closed. Selling off West View's dark attractions and roller coasters proved to be difficult. The dark attractions were later broken up, with individual scenes being sold out of Boot Hill, the once popular walk-through attraction:

> "I was (and still am) a big fan of West View Park. I have a board from The Big Dips and a piece of the center of the carousel, as well as a few signs and many smaller items. I grew up in and still live in North Hills, and the Kiddie Dips was the first coaster I ever rode as a kid. The Big Dips was the first adult coaster that I rode and Racing Whippet was the second. Fortunately, I was always tall for my age, otherwise the park may have closed before I got to ride those two. I remember the entire park in intricate detail—at least as it existed in its final years."
>
> *–Bill Linkenheimer, Ross Township, PA*

Bud Vettel took the closing of West View Park personally. His daughter Kathy said her father was never the same after the park closed and grieved losing the roller coasters and buildings his father and family designed and built. She explained years later that her son was proud of his grandfather's and family's

Using brake levers, a ride operator would manually pull a lever to slow down the train arriving back into the station.
The Brake Operator is seen sitting to the right of the train.

George Harton III was fond of the goat and featured it in park advertisements

involvement in roller coaster design and legacy. It was through Kathy's son that her father was able to relive his years in the amusement industry:

> "Our son (Rob Hilton IV) has always loved roller coasters. While living in Altoona, PA, we would take Rob to Kennywood and he and my husband, Bob, would stand in line at every roller coaster. Rob even worked at Lakemont Park on the Skyliner, making it the fourth generation of my family to work in the amusement industry. He felt connected to his grandfather and great grandfather by working on the roller coasters. On occasion, he did operate Leap the Dips. Rob is so proud and was close with his grandfather. They were very close. My dad called him Schultz."

Life After Amusements

As rides and buildings stood vacant, unwelcome visitors found their way into the now abandoned amusement park. Because West View Park was never entirely gated, the park was open to anyone. People from the community could walk the grounds at any time. This accessibility opened the door for looters and vandals, and many of the park buildings were victimized by vandals and arsonists, including the Pony Barn, Haunted House, and Boot Hill. The park staffed night security to walk the grounds; however, that did not stop someone from setting fire to one of the last standing landmarks of the park: the Dips.

On a Sunday evening in September 1980, an arsonist set fire to the Dips roller coaster. The fire is believed to have been the most intense blaze set at the park after its closing. Just like when Danceland burned to the ground in 1973, the West View community watched as years of happy memories went up in smoke. For many Pittsburghers, it was their first roller coaster. The Dips was a thriller, the most spectacular attraction at West View Park. Six fire departments fought the fire for five and a half hours, making it the most memorable fire at the park since Danceland and officially marked the end of an era. Following the Dips fire, the borough requested the remaining structures be removed from the site as soon as possible to avoid further issues. One of the last structures to be torn down was the carousel building, the only remaining structure in the park from the inaugural 1906 season. An attempt to save and repurpose the carousel building failed. The entire property was repurposed by a developer removing or leveling many of the hills. The name of the West View Park Shopping Center is the only reminder of the former amusement park.

When his career in the amusement industry ended, Jack Hickey found work initially selling cemetery lots and then enrolled in seminary. Hickey entered St. Vincent Seminary in Latrobe on August 30, 1982, and on May 24, 1986, he was officially ordained. At 63, he became the oldest graduate of the St. Vincent Seminary. Hickey recalled in the *Pittsburgh Press* of June 2, 1986:

> "I could have just gone ahead and retired. But I don't believe people have a right to retire if they have something they can contribute. I believe I have."

The West View Park Shopping Center is now located on the site formerly occupied by West View Park. The road turning into the complex is called West View Park Drive.

Although he was no longer involved in the day-to-day operations of an amusement park or the industry, Hickey became the chaplain of PAPA, in which he was past president in the mid-1970s. He also remained in touch with his friends and colleagues within the industry, most notably those at Kennywood.

Tough and difficult circumstances had surrounded West View Park and its future following the death of George Harton III. It is commonly believed Kennywood and other parks such as Geauga Lake and Cedar Point pushed West View to close; however, that was not the case. After the passing of T.M. Harton, the West View Park Company was owned equally by the remaining Harton siblings: George, Olive, and Jessie. During the 1940s, and prior to the appointment of George Harton III as president of the T.M. Harton Company, a family dispute occurred between members of the Harton family, leaving Carice Kountz as the majority stockholder in West View Park Company. But Charles Beares III, Janet Von Twistern, and Dr. George Harton IV explained a lot of secrecy surrounded their family during this time frame. A fracture occurred between family members, with the Beares family being voted out of power at West View Park.

Like many family businesses, the company was unable to make the transition into the third generation. Prior to his death, George Harton III had written in his will for his children to take the reins of West View Park. In his will, Harton explained that the park was to remain in the family's control and carry on into the next generation. In the eleven years after his passing, the park remained in family control. The plan consisted of Janet taking over day-to-day operations of the park following her father's passing, something Janet was willing to do. Dr. George Harton IV said:

> "Dad didn't want to control our future. He wanted his children to control their own future. Dad's personality was to let us do what we wanted to do."

Unfortunately, Carice Kountz was not in favor of having her granddaughter, Janet, working at the park and holding a senior management position. West View Park didn't close because it was losing money or because it was poorly run; West View Park closed because the majority shareholder in the park lost hope in the park's future without her son. In addition, Carice Kountz's husband, A.E. Kountz, was in favor of closing the park. He even told Dr. George

Harton IV on multiple occasions that the amusement industry was a failing industry, which was entirely inaccurate.

Making business decisions can be difficult, and for the Harton family, closing West View Park was extremely difficult. West View Park never completed the succession plan put in place by Olive Harton Jones and later by George Harton III for his children. Losing a loved one is never easy, and the grieving process never ended for Carice Kountz. After being widowed three times and outliving both her children, she fell into a deep depression. Grandson Dr. George Harton IV recalled:

> "She grieved for the remainder of her life. She stopped leaving the house. Dad's office remained untouched until the park closed. His name was still on the door on the final day."

Janet Von Twistern shared what her father used to say:

> "Why would I buy the place if I'll inherit the park?"

She said her father would have been better off slowly buying his mother's shares or asking her to gift him stock in the company, as it would've allowed the park to continue into the next generation easier. Dr. George Harton IV, who was called to a life of faith and ministry in 1963, remained active in West View Park Company following his father's passing by serving on the Board of Directors. His sister, Janet, also joined the Board of Directors at the same time. Harton III supported his son's decision into the life of gospel ministry and not working in the family business. Charles Beares III also explained that West View Park closed because his Aunt Carice wanted out of the business:

> "It was hard. We, Janet, George, and I, didn't want to give up on the park."

The younger generation knew the industry was changing and aggressive management by ownership was needed to sustain the park. In time, West View Park would probably still have closed due to the constant evolution and consolidation of the amusement industry. White Swan Park and Kennywood coexisted in the same market after 1977. The same could have occurred with the inclusion of West View Park.

Every year, parks must reinvent themselves with new ideas, concepts, and attractions to retain guests and make them want to return. West View Park was a sensational park; it outlasted and outperformed many parks in the industry for much of its existence. That by itself is an accomplishment that everyone who worked in, or associated with, the park should be proud to know.

T.M. Harton's Legacy Lives On

The closing of West View Park helped spark a movement outside the amusement industry. West View closed at a time when the documentation of the country's once great amusement parks started showing up in the form of newspaper articles, magazines, and book publications. The idea of documenting the history and achievements of the industry was first conceived by William F. Mangels in the early part of the twentieth century.

What used to be common practice of relocating wooden coasters in the industry began to look like a feasible and smart business decision again. The practice of relocating a wooden coaster disappeared during WWII, and for years after, seemed unfeasible. The roller coasters at West View Park stood until 1980, in hopes that a purchase offer to relocate one of the roller coasters would arise.

Fred Musso, former game concession operator at Sportland Pier in Wildwood, New Jersey, said the Ramagosa's of Sportland Pier considered relocating the Dips in 1978 after traveling to look at the ride. The ride would've been positioned so that the far turnaround would've been over the ocean. Unfortunately, the relocation project never occurred.

Dick Knoebel of Knoebel's Amusement Resort was a big fan of both coasters at West View Park and would've really wanted the Racing Whippet, because the ride was so unique. His family's park purchased the Caterpillar, stunts, equipment from the dark rides, and antique cars. The most unique purchase the Knoebel family made was a panel from West View's first carousel. The panel is now located in the Knoebel Amusement Resort Carousel Museum. Knoebel mentioned he wished he had purchased and moved one of the West View roller coasters after his family opened the Phoenix roller coaster, a wooden coaster that was relocated from another closed amusement park.

The lion and sign for the ring machine from the Waldbridge Park carousel can now be found at the Merry Go-Round Museum, Sandusky, Ohio.

A panel from West View's first carousel along with a sign reading "Return Rings Here" from West View's second carousel can now be found at Knoebels's Amusement Resort.

Unfortunately, no sale or offer was made for any of the wooden coasters. The landmark Racing Whippet and Dips roller coaster were the last rides standing until an arsonist set fire to the Dips. Following the fire, the Racing Whippet was quickly removed, followed by the remaining sections of the Dips:

"Oh, the Dips. That was everyone's favorite. Yes, this was a great place to be, really was."

–Jack Hickey

In light of West View's closing, a small group of roller coaster fans had a photo taken of them on the Racing Whippet lift hill. The photo would appear in *LIFE* magazine, accompanied by an article about a new social group, the American Coaster Enthusiasts. For seventy-one years, the city of Pittsburgh had two of the best-run amusement parks in the country. The Harton Legacy doesn't end with West View Park; it survives in many aspects, through memories, surviving parks, and individuals who want to make sure it is never forgotten. Western Pennsylvania hosted multiple amusement parks, many of which have closed. Those that survived continued to evolve, and Kennywood continues that tradition today. As the lone survivor of the local amusement park scene, Kennywood continues to entertain millions of visitors each year in a region and city that encouraged the growth and development of amusement parks. Pittsburghers are fortunate to have one of the most beloved and historic amusement parks in their hometown. More importantly, the Harton Legacy lives on at parks outside of Pennsylvania as well.

The once popular Coney Island near Cincinnati, Ohio, was reinvented as a new theme park on high ground named Kings Island, near Mason, Ohio. Gary Wachs Jr., a member of the family who owned and operated the popular Coney Island near Cincinnati, conceived Kings Island.

Wachs decided the park needed to be moved to higher ground in order to avoid flooding from the Ohio River and to allow for park expansion.

Originally, management planned to reerect the Shooting Star roller coaster from Coney Island at Kings Island but decided to build an entirely new roller coaster in a previous undeveloped section of the new property. In 1977, Andy Vettel and John Allen were asked to consult on the new roller coaster project and its design. Vettel embraced the opportunity and, in theory, continued the legacy established by T.M. Harton in the early part of the century in roller coaster construction. In a letter to Kings Island Chief Engineer Allen Collin, Vettel said, "I like your coaster very much, as it has practically everything I have or want to do in the future. High dip, camelback, spiral, blind curves, tunnels, etc." The Beast opened at Kings Island in 1979 as a the tallest, fastest, and longest wooden roller coaster. To this day, The Beast is one of the most popular rides at Kings Island and one of the most popular roller coasters in the world.

Before his retirement from Kennywood following the 1981 summer season, Andy Vettel Sr. worked on one final roller coaster at Kennywood. As the construction supervisor for the famed Laser Loop, Andy helped solidify Kennywood's claim to the title of Coaster Capital of the World. Without T.M. Harton's help, the Vettels may have never become involved or associated with so many projects that led to them being pioneers in the industry. Kennywood continues to honor that legacy and commitment to this day.

T.M. Harton showcased his roller coaster empire to the world with the Vettels as master roller coaster engineers. West View Park was at the heart of this empire and in the hearts of millions of people. Although gone, the park lives on in the memories and folklore of locals and those who knew it best. The memory and legacy of the T.M. Harton Company lives on through this book and the amusement industry it served. An empty amusement park is just a park; the buildings and amusements give it character, but the employees and patrons alike provide the magic and the memories they create. It's a magic that need never disappear. The amusement industry puts the fun in life and allows the imagination to run wild and create unforgettable memories.

West View Park was a major part of West View Borough and the surrounding community. Although people currently living in West View may never have visited the park, they are aware of the role the amusement park played in the lives of people who knew it best and most importantly: the local community:

"West View Park was an unexpected treasure during my exhaustive four-week cross-country trip in the summer of 1974, in preparation for writing The Great American Amusement Parks.

"What immediately impressed me was seeing the banked turnaround of the Dips coaster right against the highway, a wonderful surprise, a come-on, a tease for a traditional amusement park, which I soon realized was set in a small valley, enveloping the park in green. Besides the Dips, which I found to be a very nice out-and-back, there was an impressive array of standard rides, all nicely placed in and around the midway. It was truly an amusement park—a park with amusements—a place where an adult could comfortably spend the whole day while the kids rode themselves silly.

"As we proceeded westward toward the back of the park, I was astounded—yes, astounded—to see a racing coaster nestled neatly in a ravine! What a surprise, it wasn't shown on the scant brochure. To this day, the Racing Whippet is the best racer I've been on. There was certainly soul in both the park and its operation. The surprises weren't over though, as we continued north from the Racing Whippet, we saw yet a third wood coaster, a kiddie coaster, Kiddie Dips. It delivered a solid ride and was also in great shape.

"My wonderful day at West View Park will never be forgotten; I'm smiling now as I think of it, and grateful that I'm old enough to have experienced it."

–Gary Kyriazi, New River, AZ

During his lifetime, Theodore Marshall Harton was at the top of the amusement industry, building amusement rides and devices. His name and company were known throughout the United States, Canada, England, and Europe. He not only helped develop the amusement and attractions industry, he opened the door of opportunity to multiple other individuals who too made a difference in the industry. He helped create the amusement park industry, connecting people and employees to provide memorable experiences all over the world. Theodore Harton was a true pioneer who inspired others to move the industry forward. His impact is still felt today and is carried on by people who might not even be aware of his name.

Established in 1990, the IAAPA Hall of Fame celebrates outstanding individuals whose achievements and contributions led to the growth and development of the amusement park and attractions industry. In honor of his accomplishments and significant contributions to the industry, Theodore Harton was inducted posthumously into the IAAPA Hall of Fame in 1994. It was fitting that T.M. Harton was inducted into the Hall of Fame by Carl Hughes, then acting chairman of the Hall of Fame Committee and executive of longtime Pittsburgh competitor Kennywood. To begin the ceremony, Hughes said:

> "Welcome to the 1994 Hall of Fame Awards. We have some outstanding people to induct this year, some that have made major changes and contributions to this industry."

Accepting the award at the 1994 ceremony was T.M. Harton's great niece, Janet Harton Von Twistern.

> "I think you all are in a wonderful business. What a life. To make so many people so happy, it's such an honor to accept this. Thank you very much."

And as the ride comes to a complete stop, take time to be thankful and smile, because what makes any park special are the memories. And those memories will last a lifetime.

"And could we just have one more applause for our living legend and our legends of the past. Thank You!"

–Carl Hughes

Just prior to the turn of the twentieth century, T.M. Harton set his sights on making a difference in entertainment. Harton was an amusement industry pioneer who helped establish Pittsburgh as the training ground for future roller coaster builders, engineers, and industry professionals. The founding of West View Park reaffirmed his commitment to family entertainment and long-term success of the amusement park industry.

"We here at West View Park sincerely hope you had a most enjoyable day with us. As West View Park closes for the evening, we would once again like to thank you for your patronage today and extend to you a most cordial invitation to return again during this 1977 season. And now, on behalf of the staff and management at West View Park, we bid you all a most pleasant good night.

–Skip Morrow, Operations Manager and the "Voice" of West View Park

Even in the later years, West View Park still transformed into a magical place at night with its neon and ride lights.

Along with red arrows, directional stickers were commonly found on telephone poles

This themed furniture was previously located in the administration office

Over a decade after the parks final season, former employees gathered to remember and celebrate the legacy of West View Park

The Racing Whippet was considered a mobius racing coaster, meaning the ride is considered one long loop with one train started on one side, and ending on the opposite side it started.

The Kennywood Jack Rabbit features three trains designed by Edward Vettel Sr. The original Vettel Jack Rabbit trains were built in the West View Park cafeteria before being shipped to Kennywood. Each offseason, West View Park's cafeteria became a maintenance workshop for various offseason projects. The Thunderbolt, designed by Andy Vettel Sr., is considered one of the best and most popular wooden roller coasters in the amusement industry. For many, it will always be Kennywood's top wooden roller coaster.

The parking lots located next to Center Avenue, are now occupied by apartments. A tunnel used to take guests under center avenue from the parking lots and guests would enter in front of Danceland. Located on Center Avenue, Center Slice Pizza features this mural on the side of the building dedicated to West View Park.

Appendices

T.M. Harton Company Presidents (1893-1982)

Theodore M. Harton II 1893-1919
George M. Harton II 1919-1920
Olive Harton Jones 1920-1945
George M. Harton III 1946-1966
A.E. Kountz 1966-1975
Margaret S. Habel 1975-1980

Parks owned by T.M. Harton Company (1902-1980)

Walbridge Park.. 1902-1957 (1964-Property sold)
Athletic Park/Luna Park .... 1905-1909 (Park sold)
West View Park... 1905-1980 (1977-Park closure)

T.M. Harton Company - business accounts / subsidiary companies

Buckroe Beach Toboggan Company
Bug Washington D.C.
Carousel Construction

Cedar Point Toboggan Company
Cedar Point Carousel & Building

Celeron Toboggan
Celeron Carousel

Coney Island Carousel & Building
Coney Island Dips Company

Bingo Conneaut
Conneaut-Idlewild Company
Conneaut Lake Park Convention Hall Company
Conneaut Lake Park Company
Conneaut Lake Rides Company
Conneaut Lake Toboggan Company
Exposition Park Scenic Railway Company
Exposition Park Toboggan Construction

Clason Point Toboggan Company

Exposition Park Carousel
Exposition Park Toboggan

Forest Hill Park Toboggan Company

Glen Island Dips Company
Globe Theatre Company
Harton Scenic Railway Company Limited
Highland Park Toboggan Company

Harton and Salsbury Stocks
    Kennywood Racing Coaster Company
    Oil City Coaster Company
    Anderson Coaster Company
    Ingersoll Engineering Company
    Newburg Amusement Company
    Josiah Pearce & Sons

Harton Theatre Company Inc.
North Side Amusement Company
Novelty Theatre Company

Idlewild Carousel

Idora Park Carousel & Building
Idora Park Toboggan Company

International Amusement Company
Island Park Toboggan Company
Josiah Pearce & Sons Company
King Edward Park Toboggan Company
Long Branch Toboggan Company
Luna Park Toboggan Company of Schenectady
Marshall Hall Park Toboggan Company
Manchester Toboggan Slide Company

Oakford Park Carousel & Building
Oakford Park Toboggan

Olympia Park Toboggan & Carousel

Paxtang Park Toboggan Company

Paterson Toboggan Company
Riji Beach Toboggan Company
Southern Park Toboggan Co

Tickets and Rings
Toronto Scenic Dips Company

Toboggan Construction
Toboggan Amusement Company

Toledo Beach Toboggan Company
Toledo Beach Toboggan Construction
Toledo Beach Carousel Company

Uniontown Speedway Association

Waldameer Park Toboggan Company
Waldameer Park House of Hilarity

Walbridge Park Amusement Company
    Walbridge Park Caterpillar Company
    Walbridge Park Caroussel Company
    Walbridge Park Cuddle Up Company
    Walbridge Park Skooter Company
    Walbridge Park Toboggan Company
    Walbridge Park Toboggan Construction
    Walbridge Park Old Mill Company
    Walbridge Park Refreshment Company
    Walbridge Park Coliseum Company

West View Park Company
    West View Park Refreshment Company
    West View Park Whip Company
    Racing Whippet Company
    Racing Whippet Construction
    West View Dips Company
    West View Greyhound Company

Wolverine Amusement Company
    Wolverine Bug Company

Zarro-Unger Construction Company

Harton Concessions

Park	Location
Athletic Park/Luna Park	Buffalo, NY
Avon Park	Youngstown, PA
Bluegrass Park	Lexington, KY
Scenic/Casino	Toledo, OH
Cedar Point	Sandusky, OH
Celeron Park	Jamestown, NY
Coney Island	Cincinnati, OH
Conneaut Lake Park	Conneaut Lake, PA
Crystal Beach	Ontario, CAN
Crystal Beach Park	Vermillion, OH
Dominion Park	Montreal, CAN
Eldridge Park	Elmira, New York
Electric Park	Detroit, MI
Electric Park	Newark, NJ
Electric Park	Albany, NY
Fairyland Park	Paterson, NJ
Ferncliffe Park/Avon Park	Girard, OH
Glen Haven Park	Rochester, NY
Lakeside Park/Enna Jettick Park	Auburn, NY

T.M. Harton Company Roller Coasters (Chronologically)

list includes roller projects completed by Vettel Family

Ride	Park	Location	Years Operated
Switchback Railway/ Gravity Railroad (Griffith & Crane Scenic & Gravity Railroad)	Pittsburgh Exposition	Pittsburgh, Pennsylvania	1895-1900
Scenic Figure 8 Railway (Griffith & Crane Scenic & Gravity Railroad)	Walbridge Park	Toledo, Ohio	1899-1915
Figure Eight/ Toboggan Run	Pittsburgh Exposition	Pittsburgh, Pennsylvania	1901-1916
Scenic Auto-Dip	Canadian National Exposition (CNE)	Toronto, Ontario, Canada	1902-1907
Figure Eight	Waldameer Park	Erie, Pennsylvania	1902-1937
Figure Eight (Ingersoll) #1	Exposition Park	Conneaut Lake, Pennsylvania	1902-1908, 1909-1921
Figure Eight (Ingersoll – Erwin Vettel)	Kennywood Park	West Mifflin, Pennsylvania	1902-1921
Figure Eight (Ingersoll – John Miller, Erwin Vettel)	Seabreeze Amusement Park	Rochester, New York	1903-1915
Figure Eight	Celoron Park	Jamestown, New York	1903-1932
Figure Eight	Ramona Park	East Grand Rapids, Michigan	1903-1913
Figure Eight	Eldridge Park	Elmira, New York	1903-?
Figure Eight	Rorick's Glen Park	Elmira, New York	1903-1918
Unknown Name	Rye Beach	Rye, New York	?-?
Unknown Name	Riverside Park	Montreal Canada	?-?

Figure Eight	Atlantic City Boardwalk	Atlantic City, NJ	1903-1905 (early 1900s)
Toboggan Slide	Ferncliffe Park/Avon Park	Girad, Ohio	1904-1920s
Figure Eight (Ingersoll)	Athletic Park	Buffalo, New York	1904-1909
Figure Eight	Junction Park	Beaver, Pennsylvania	1904-1907
Figure Eight	Crystal Beach Park	Niagara Falls, Canada	1905-1915
Figure Eight (Griffith & Crane Scenic & Gravity Railway)	Olympic Park	Newark, New Jersey	1905-1920
Figure Eight	Rocky Springs Park	Lancaster, Pennsylvania	1905-1917
Figure Eight/ Coaster Flyer	Paxtang Park	Harrisburg, Pennsylvania	1905-1922
Figure Eight (Harton/Pearce)	Fairyland Park	Paterson, New Jersey	1905-1910
Figure Eight (Griffith & Crane Scenic & Gravity Railway)	Glen Haven Park	Rochester, New York	1906-1909
Scenic Railway (Griffith & Crane Scenic & Gravity Railway)	Dominion Park	Montreal, Canada	1906-1919
Figure Eight (Griffith & Crane Scenic & Gravity Railway)	Luna Park/Dolle's Park/ Rexford Park	Schenectady, New York	1906-1910
Figure Eight	Long Branch Park	Geddas, New Jersey	1906-1925
Figure Eight/Speedway	Oakford Park	Jeannette, Pennsylvania	1906-1940
Figure Eight (#1)	West View Park	West View, Pennsylvania	1906-1908
Toboggan	White City Park	Manchester, England	1907-?
Figure Eight	Southern Park	Pittsburgh, Pennsylvania	1907-1910
Figure Eight	Coney Island (Ohio)	Cincinnati, Ohio	1907-1918
Dip the Dips	Waldameer Park	Erie, Pennsylvania	1907-1937

Scenic Figure Eight (Griffith & Crane Scenic & Gravity Railway)	Highland Park	York, Pennsylvania	1907-1916?
Figure Eight (Griffith & Crane Scenic & Gravity Railway)	Island Park	Easton, Pennsylvania	1907-1920
Figure 8 Toboggan (Erwin Vettel)	Belle Vue Park	England	1908-?
Auto Dips / Scenic Railway	Athletic Park	Buffalo, New York	1908-1909
Scenic Railway (Griffith & Crane Scenic & Gravity Railway)	Electric Park	Albany (Kinderhook Lake), New York	1908-1920?
Figure Eight (Griffith & Crane Scenic & Gravity Railway)	Palisades Park	Cliffside Park-Fort Lee, New Jersey	1908-?
Dip The Dips Scenic Railway	Cedar Point	Sandusky, Ohio	1908-1917
Figure Eight (Griffith & Crane Scenic & Gravity Railway)	Bayonne Point Pleasure Park	Bayonne, New Jersey	1909-?
Figure Eight (#2)	West View Park	West View, Pennsylvania	1909-1926
$25,000 Ride (#1)	West View Park	West View, Pennsylvania	1909-1912
Scenic Railway	Conneaut Lake Park	Conneaut Lake, Pennsylvania	1909-1936
Unknown Name (Griffith & Crane Scenic & Gravity Railway)	Schuetzen Park	Union Hil, New Jersey	?-?
Unknown Name (Griffith & Crane Scenic & Gravity Railway)		Hoboken, New Jersey	?-?
Scenic Railway (Griffith & Crane Scenic & Gravity Railway)	Clason Point Park	Clason Point, New York	1910-1927/1935?
Dips/Roller Dips/ Jack Rabbit	Buckroe Beach Park	Hampton, Virginia	1910-1921

Harton Scenic Railway	Kursaal	England	1910-1973
Dip The Dips	Cleethropes, England	Cleethropes, England	1910s
Unknown Name (Erwin Vettel)	Brussells, Belgium	Brussells, Belgium	1910s
Figure 8 Bahn	Munich, Germany	Munich, Germany	1910s
Unknown Name (Erwin Vettel)	Munich, Germany	Munich, Germany	1910s
Firgure Eight	Ausstellung Wiesbaden Fair Germany		1910s
Unknown Name (Erwin Vettel)		Blackpool, England	1910s
Racing Dips	King Edwards Amusement Park	Boucherville, Quebec, Canada	1911-1928
Dip the Dips	Luna Park/Dolle's Park/ Rexford Park	Schenectady, New York	1911-1917
Dips	Glen Island Park	New Rochelle, New York	1911-1920
Derby Racer (Miller - Pearce/Harton, Erwin Vettel)	Revere Beach	Revere, Massachusetts	1911-1936
Dip the Dips	Coney Island	Cincinnati, Ohio	1911-1918
Little Dipper	Coney Island	Cincinnati, Ohio	1912-1918
Leap The Dips	Cedar Point	Sandusky, Ohio	1912-1935
Leap-the-Dips (#2)	West View Park	West View, Pennsylvania	1913-1919
Dip-The-Dips	Idora Park	Youngstown, Ohio	1914-1923
Trip Thru the Clouds (Keenan - Pearce/ Harton)	Electric Park	Detroit, Michigan	1915-1924
Figure Eight	Lakeside Park/Enna Jettick Park	Auborn, New York	1916?-1924
Toboggan	Walbridge Park	Toledo, Ohio	1916-1928
Dips/Greyhound	Seabreeze Amusement Park	Rochester, New York	1916-1930
Giant Coaster	Crystal Beach Park	Niagara Falls, Canada	1916-1989

Speed-O-Plane	West View Park	West View, Pennsylvania	1917-1927
Leap Frog Railway	Cedar Point	Sandusky, Ohio	1918-1933
Dip the Dips	Coney Island	Cincinnati, Ohio	1918-1928
Leap-the-Dips (#3)	West View Park	West View, Pennsylvania	1919-1928
Toboggan	Marshall Hall Park	Bryans, Maryland	1921-1931
Toboggan	Toledo Beach	Toledo Beach, Michigan	1917?1921?-1941
Jack Rabbit (#2)	Conneaut Lake Park	Conneaut Lake, Pennsylvania	1922-1935
Jack Rabbit	Idora Park	Youngstown, Ohio	1924-1984
Giant Racer (Erwin Vettel)	Pleasure Park	Redcar, England	1925-1937
Sky Rocket (Miller – Erwin Vettel)	Palisades Park	Cliffside Park-Fort Lee, New Jersey	1926-1944
Big Dipper (Erwin Vettel)	Wonderland Amusement Park		1926-1944
Racing Whippet	West View Park	West View, Pennsylvania	1927-1977
Greyhound	West View Park	West View, Pennsylvania	1928-1945
Crystal Flyer/Thriller	Crystal Beach Park	Vermillion, Ohio	1928-1962
Dips	West View Park	West View, Pennsylvania	1929-1977
Whoopie Speedway / Speedway	Walbridge Park	Toledo, Ohio	1929-1937
Thunderbolt (Ed Vettel - NAD)	Willow Grove Park	Willow Grove, Pennsylvania	1931-1975
High Frolics	Cedar Point	Sandusky, Ohio	1934-1940
Kiddie Coaster	Idora Park	Youngstown, Ohio	1936-1984
Blue Streak	Conneaut Lake Park	Conneaut Lake, Pennsylvania	1937-2022
Giant Racer (Erwin Vettel)	Sheerness Amusement Park		1938

Ride	Park	Location	Years Operated
Zephyr (Ed Vettel - NAD)	Pontchartrain Beach Park	New Orleans, Lousianna	1939-1983
Cyclone (Ed Vettel & Sons)	Lakeside Amusement Park	Denver, Colorado	1940-Present
Kiddie Dips	West View Park	West View, Pennsylvania	1949-1977
Bomber (Vettel - NAD)	Rainbow Gardens	White Oak, Pennsylvania	1954-1968

Ride	Park	Location	Years Operated
Little Dipper/Dipper (Andy Vettel)	Kennywood Park	West Mifflin, Pennsylvania	1948-1983
Thunderbolt (John Miller - Andy Vettel/ John Allen)	Kennywood Park	West Mifflin, Pennsylvania	1968-Present
Laser Loop (Anton Schwarzkopf)	Kennywood Park	West Mifflin, Pennsylvania	1980-1990
The Beast (Al Collins, Jeff Ranke, John Allen)	Kings Island	Kings Mill, Ohio	1979-Present

Harton & Salsbury Roller Coasters

Purchased when T.M. Harton Company Acquired Ingersoll Engineering &
Construction Company in 1918

Ride	Park	Location	Years Operated
Giant Safety Coaster (Miller - Ingersoll Co)	Forest Hill Park	Chicago, Illinois	1908-1918/1921
Leap The Dips (Miller - Ingersoll Co)	Forest Hill Park	Chicago, Illinois	1908-1918/1922
Leap-The-Dips (Miller - Ingersoll Co)	Mounds Park	Anderson, Indiana	1908-1928/1929
Scenic Railway (Miller - Ingersoll Co - Pearce, Erwin Vettel)	Bluegrass Park	Lexington, Kentucky	1910-1925
Racer (Miller - Ingersoll Co)	Kennywood Park	West Mifflin, Pennsylvania	1910-1926
Leap The Dips (Miller - Ingersoll Co - Pearce, Erwin Vettel)	Ocean View Park	Norfolk, Virginia	1910-1928
Speed-o-Plane (Miller - Ingersoll Co)	Kennywood Park	West Mifflin, Pennsylvania	1911-1923
Thriller (Miller - Ingersoll Co)	Monarch Park	Oil City, Pennsylvania	1913-1926
Giant Racer (Miller - Ingersoll Co)	Savin Rock Park	West Haven, Connecticut	1914-1927

West View Park Rides

Ride	Manufacturer	Years Operated
Alpine Sky Ride	John T. Gibbs Ltd.	1965-1977
Antique Cars	Arrow Development	1963-1977
Auto Scooters (New Cars 1935, 1952, 1964, 1975)	Lusse Brothers	1926-1977
Bantem Tractors	Trebron	1954-1969?
Bicycle Ride (Kiddie Ride)	West View Park Co.	1958-1965?
Boot Hill	Bill Tracy/Outdoor Dimensional Design	1964-1977
Bump the Bumps	T.M. Harton Company	1906-1909
Cadillac Cars (Kiddie Ride)		1955-1977
Carousel #1	Dentzel/Harton	1906-1913
Carousel #2	Muller/Harton	1914-1977
Carousel #3	Muller/Harton	1923-1943
Caterpillar #1	Traver Engineering	1924-1956
Caterpillar #2	Allan Herschell Company	1957-1977
Chair Plane	Smith & Smith Company	1944-1973
Cuddle-Up	PTC/Berk Engineering	1930-1963
Davey Jones Locker	R.E. Chambers/Outdoor Dimensional Design	1964-1976
Ferris Wheel #1	T.M. Harton Company	1911-1945
Ferris Wheel #2	Eli-Bridge Company	1946-1968
Flying Scooter	Bisch-Rocco Company	1946-1977
Frazzle House (Funhouse)	T.M. Harton Company	1914-?
Hand Cars (Kiddie Ride)	Hodge Amusements	1954-1977
Hale's Tour of the World		1906-?
Haunted House	Allan Herschell/Outdoor Dimension Design	1963-1977
Haunted Swing	West View Park Co.	1956-1963

House of Enchantment (Funhouse)	T.M. Harton Company	1914
Helicopters	Allan Herschell Company	1958-1977
Hilarity Hall/House (Funhouse)	T.M. Harton Company	1915-1931
Jolly Caterpillar (Kiddie Ride)	Allan Herschell Company	1964-1977
Joy Plane	Aero Joy Plane Company	1923-1928
Katzenjammer Castle (Funhouse)	T.M. Harton Company	1907-1914
Kiddie Auto Ride	Allan Herschell Company	1947?-1977
Kiddie Boats	Allan Herschell Company	1940s-1977
Kiddie Bug	R.E. Chambers Company	1950-1977
Kiddie Car Ride		?-1944?
Kiddie Carousel	W.F Mangels Company	1944-1977
Miniature Airplane (Circle Swing)	W.F Mangels Company	1943-1977
Kiddie Ferris Wheel	W.F Mangels Company	1941-1977
Kiddie Jeep Ride	Allan Herschell Company	1951-?
Kiddie Paddle Boat	Allan Herschell Company	1958-?
Kiddie Whip	W.F. Mangels Company	1941-1977
Krazy Dazy Orbit (Scrambler)	Eli-Bridge Company	1962-1977
Land of the Giants	R.E. Chambers Company/ ?	1977
Loop-O-Plane #1	Eyerly Aircraft Company	1936-1948
Loop-O-Plane #2	Eyerly Aircraft Company	1949-1954
Looper	Allan Herschell Company	1958-1964
Magic Carpet/Bat Chute	Ben Schiff	1961-1977
Miniature Golf / Contour Golf / Goofy Golf	Holmes Cook	1952-1977
Miniature Train #1 (Fledgling Flyer)	National Amusement Device	1946-1969
Miniature Train #2 (C.p. Huntington - 79)	Chance Manufacturing	1970-1977
Mirror Maze		1954-1963
Moon Rocket #1 (Rocket)	Allan Herschell Company	1941-1955
Moon Rocket #2	Allan Herschell Company	1960-1963
Mystic Chutes	T.M. Harton Company	1906-1914

Paratrooper (Hydraulic Model)	Frank Hrubetz	1971-1977
Pony Carts (Kiddie Ride)	W.F. Mangels Company	1941-1977
Pony Track	T.M. Harton Company	1906-1977
Ride-N-Laff	R.E. Chambers Company	1938-1963
Razzle Dazzle	T.M. Harton Company	1907-1908
Rodeo (Kiddie Ride)	Allan Herschell Company	1964-1977
Rock-O-Plane	Eyerly Aircraft Company	1958-1977
Fairy Whip (Roto Whip)	W.F. Mangels Company	1941-1977
Rotor	Anglo-Rotor	1957
Round Up #1	Frank Hrubetz	1958-1962
Round Up #2 (Trailer Mount)	Frank Hrubetz	1967-1977
Row Boats		1906-1950s
Scoota Boats		1940-1963
Sky Fighter (Kiddie Ride)	Allan Herschell Company	1952-1977
Sky Wheel	Allan Herschell Company	1969-1970
Strato-Ship	R.E. Chambers Company	1939-1943
Tempest	Grover-Watkins	1974-1977
Tilt-A-Whirl #1	Sellner Manufacturing	1948-1967
Tilt-A-Whirl #2	Sellner Manufacturing	1968-1977
Trabant	Chance Manufacturing	1965-1977
Tumble Bug (Bug)	Traver Engineering	1929-1977
Up-C-Daze (Flying Cages)	B.A. Schiff	1963-1966
Water Scooters	Lusse Brothers	1935-1939
Whip #1	W.F. Mangels Company	1919-1937
Whip #2	W.F. Mangels Company	1938-1977

West View Park Roller Coasters

Ride	Manufacturer	Years Operated
Figure Eight (#1)	Ed Vettel/T.M. Harton Co	1906-1908
Figure Eight/Roller Coaster/ Toboggan (#2)	Ed Vettel/T.M. Harton Co	1909-1926
$25,000 Ride (#1)	Ed Vettel/T.M. Harton Co	1910-1912
Leap-the-Dips (#2)	Ed Vettel/T.M. Harton Co	1913-1919
Dip-the-Dips (#3)	Ed Vettel/T.M. Harton Co	1919-1922
Dip-the-Dips (#4)	Ed Vettel/T.M. Harton Co	1923-1928
Dips (#5)	Ed Vettel/T.M. Harton Co	1929-1977
Speed-O-Plane (#1)	Ed Vettel/T.M. Harton Co	1917-1927
Greyhound (#2)	Ed Vettel/T.M. Harton Co	1928-1945
Racing Whippet	Ed Vettel/T.M. Harton Co	1927-1977
Kiddie Dips	Ed Vettel/T.M. Harton Co	1949-1977
Brownie Coaster	W.F. Mangels Company	1943-1960s
Wild Mouse	Imported from Germany	1961-1962

West View Park Marketing/Advertising Slogans

1920s . . . . West View Park – The Park of a Thousand Trees
1931 . . . . West View Park – Just For Fun
1938 . . . . West View Park – Breeze Cooled!
1941 . . . . West View Park – Just For Fun
1943 . . . . West View Park – Pittsburgh's Most Natural Playground
1945 . . . . .West View Park – Just For Fun and Relaxation
1946 - 1948 . . . . West View Park – For a Good Time, All the Time
1949 . . . . This Year it's West View Park
1949 - 1965 . . . . West View Park – An Amusement Park of Rare Beauty
1955 . . . . West View Park 50th Anniversary
1960-66 . . . . .West View Park – Pittsburgh's Most Popular Playground
1967 . . . . .Action! West View Park
1968 . . . . "Action" Attractions West View Park
1969 . . . . West View the Fun Park
1970 - 1973 . . . . .West View Park – The Fun Park
1973 . . . . Rediscover the Excitement... West View Park
1974 . . . . West View "The Fun Park"
1977 . . . . West View Park – The Fun Park Pittsburgh's Favorite Playground

West View Park Company Presidents (1906-1977)

Theodore M. Harton II 1906-1919
George M. Harton II 1919-1920
Charles L. Beares Sr. 1920-1946
George M. Harton III 1946-1966
A.E. Kountz 1966-1975
Margaret S. Habel 1975-1977

West View Park General Managers (1906-1977)

Oliver MacKalip . . . . 1906-1913 (VP & GM)
J.H. Maxwell 1913-1918
F.H. Tooker 1919-1924
Howell C. Beares 1925-1930
Frank L. Danahey 1931-1932
Charles L. Beares Jr. . . . . 1926-1932 (Assistant GM)
Charles L. Beares Jr. . . . . 1933-1946 (VP & GM)

George M. Harton III .... 1946-1966 (President & GM)
    George Bodnar .... 1960-1966 (Assistant GM)
    John (Jack) Hickey Jr.. .... 1960-1966 (Assistant GM)
John (Jack) P. Hickey Jr.. .... 1966-1977 (VP & GM)
    Tom "Skip" Morrow .... 1974-1976 (Assistant GM)

West View Park Maintenance Superintendent (1906-1977)

Edward A. Vettel 1906-1952
    Edward E. Vettel .... 1947-1952 (Assistant Superintendent)
Edward E. Vettel 1952-1964
    Robert W. Vettel .... 1952-1964 (Assistant Superintendent)
Robert W. Vettel 1964-1977

West View Park Dance Pavilion / Danceland Managers (1906-1973)

Charles "Chick" Saunders .... 1934-?
Bill Bodan .... ?-1944
Jack Stoll 1944-1964
Jackie Weisser 1946-1961
George Bodnar 1961-1966
Tom "Skip" Morrow". 1967-1973

Promotion & Picnic Days at West View Park (partial list)

13Q Radio Day
14K Music Radio Day
Adams Township
All Saint's Church
Allegheny Vocational School
Allis Chalmers Company
American Bridge
Aspinwall Schools
Assumption School
Avalon School District
Avonworth School
Babcock School District
Barbershop Quartet Day
Beechview Schools
Bellevue Schools
Bethlehem Steel Company
Boggs & Buhls Department Store
Brookline Community Day
Brookline Schools
Cannon-McMillan School District
Catholic Nun's Day
Carpenters Union
Chartiers Township Day
Clayton School
Coca-Coca Fun Day
Coca-Cola Company
Country Western Music Days
Crucible Steel Company
Dollar Bank Day
Duquesne Heights
    Civic Association
East End Community Day
East End Day
East North Side Business Men
East Park Community Day
Emsworth Public Schools

Equitable Gas Company
Etna Public Schools
Eureka Life Insurance Company
Federal Enameling and
    Stamping Company
Festival of Fire
Fineview Community Day
Firework Days
First United Evangelical
    Protestant Church
    (North Side)
Fox Chapel School District
Fraternal Order of Police Officers
Freedom Area Schools
French-Belgian Club
Gimbels Department Store
Glenshaw Glass
Guardian Angel's Church
    (West End)
H.J. Heinz Company
Hamfest-Ham Radio Operators
Heppenstall
Hill District Community Day
Hill District Day
Holy Family (Lawrenceville)
Holy Name Church
Holy Rosary Roman Catholic
    Church (Homewood)
Holy Sepulchaer Schools Picnic
Horace Mann School
Idora Park Employees
Immaculate Heart
    Catholic Church
Irish Day
Iron Worker Local 3
Ironworkers Union

Italian Day
J&L Steel
John M. Controy School
Junior Commandos Picnic
Knights of Columbus
Knoxville Schools
KQV Radio Appreciation Day /
    KQV Family Day
Latimer Junior High
Lincoln Lemington
    Community Day
Lincoln-Larimar Community
    Picnic Day
Linwood School
Local 211 Carpenters
Lockhart Community Day
Manchester School
Mars Area School District
McNaughter School
Mellon Bank
Mesta Machine Company
Middlesex Area School District
Milk Drivers' Union
Mine Safety Appliance
Moon School District
Mothers of Fifteenth Engineers
National Junior Miss America
    Contest
National Kiddies Day
Nativity Catholic Church
    (Northside)
Nativity Grade School
Neville School District
Newspaper Day
North Allegheny School District
North Hills School District

Northside Community Day
Northside Day
Oakland Board of Trade
One Price Day
Order of Independent Americans
Order of the Eastern Star
    Home Association
Overbrook Schools
Owen-Illinois Can Company
Pittsburgh & Lake Erie
    Employees and Family Day
Pittsburgh Chemical Company
Pittsburgh City Firefighters
Pittsburgh Forgings Company
The Pittsburgh Press
Plum Borough
Polish Day
Polish Falcons
The Press Boys & Girls Club
Quaker Valley
    School District
Reel Family Reunion
Retail Butchers & Meat Dealers
    Association
Richland School District
Saraha Temple
Schiller Community Day
Seckatary Hawkins Club
Secks's American Rangers and
    Rangerettes
Shaler Township Public Schools
Sharpsburg Public Schools
Sons and Daughters of Liberty
South Hills Community Day
South Hills Day
Spring Gardens Schools
St. Adelbert's Roman Catholic
    Church (South Side)
St. Alphonsus School (Wexford)
St. Anne's Roman Catholic
    Church (Millvale)

St. Anthony's Catholic Church
    (Millvale)
St. Augustine Church
St. Boniface
St. Catherine School (Wildwood)
St. Cyril
St. Felix School (Freedom)
St. Frances deSales
    (McKees Rocks)
St. Francis Xavier
St. Gabriel's Church
St. George School (Allentown)
St. Hyacinth's Church (Craft
    Avenue)
St. Ignatius Church (Carnegie)
St. James Roman Catholic
    Church (West End)
St. John the Baptist Roman
    Catholic Church
    (Lawrenceville)
St. Justin (Mt. Washington)
St. Kieran's Church
St. Leo's (Northside)
St. Louise deMarillac School
St. Martin's Church (West End)
St. Mary's (Carnegie)
St. Mary's (Lawrenceville)
St. Mary's (Sharpsburg)
St. Nicholas School (Northside)
St. Norbert's School
St. Peter's Lutheran Church
    (Northside)
St. Phillips
St. Philomena's Catholic Church
St. Richard's Church
St. Rosalia's Roman Catholic
    Church (Greenfield Avenue)
St. Stephen's Roman Catholic
    Church (Hazelwood)
St. Teresa
St. Ursula Church (Allison Park)

Teamsters 249
Thorofare Days –
    22 Years est. 1955
Troy Hill Community Day
Ukrainian Day
United Food and Commercial
    Workers 1407
United Labor League of Western
    Pennsylvania
United States Post Office
United Sunday Schools of
    Sheriden
Valencia School District
VFW West View Picnic
Wean United
Weep Day
West Deer School Picnic
West End Community Day
West End Day
West End School District
West View Highland Games-
    Scotch Day
West View School District
Western and Southern
    Insurance Company
Westwood Public Schools
Westwood Public Schools
WIIC-NBC TV Family Day
Williams Company
Winter Carnival

Condensed list of Bands, Orchestras, Artists who played at West View Park

Al Powell & His Dixeland Six
Andy Williams
Artie Arnell & Orchestra
Baron Elliott's Orchestra
Barry Blue's Orchestra
The Beach Boys
Benny Goodman
Bill Haley & The Comets
Bobby Comstock
Bobby Dale
Bobby Darin
Bobby Goldsboro
Bobby Randell
Bobby Vinton
Buddy Lee's Orchestra
Buddy Morrow & Orchestra
Cally Dodd
Cecil Barber
Charlie Shavers
The Chiffons
The Chimes
Chubby Checker
Clyde Knight Orchestra
Curtis Elliott
Danny Nirella's Band
Dave Clark Five
Dion & The Belmonts
Duane Eddy & the Rebels
The Duprees
Eddie Hidge
Endland Dan & John Ford Coley
Florraine Darlin
The Four Freshmen
Frank Jarema's Orchestra
Frank Sinatra Jr.
Frank Wajnarowski

Frankie Yankovic
Freddy Cannon
Gene Krupa & Orchestra
Gene McDaniels
Gene Pitney
Gene Vincent & His Blue Caps
Gene Williams Orchestra
Glenn Lads Orchestra
Glenn Miller Orchestra
Grand Army Band
Gus Dolfi & the Horizon
        Room Orchestra
Guy Lombardo
Harold Betters
Harry James
Helen Forrest
Izzy Cervone's Band
James Brown
Jan & Dean
Johnny & the Hurricanes
Johnny Daye
Johnny Hyzny
Johnny Jack
Johnny Maestro
Joni Wilson's Debonairs
Ken Francis Orchestra
Kenny Bass & Polka Orchestra
Larry Verne
Lee Kelton Orchestra
Les Brown
Little Anthony & the Imperials
Louis Prima & Keely Smith
Marcy Jo
Marty Schramm & his Ochestra
Men of Chantz
Mirriam Johnson

Nancy Fingal
Neil Sedaka
Paul & Paula
Paul Revere and The Raiders
The Pied Pipers
The Pixie's Three
Ralph Flanagan
Ralph Harrison & Orchestra
The Regents
The Rolling Stones
Russ Morgan & Orchestra
Russ Romero & Orchestra
The Secrets
Shangri-Las
Skip & Flip
Skyliners
Slim Bryant & the Wildcats
Sonny James
Stan Kenton
Sunshine Boys
Tex Beneke
Tommy & Jimmy Dorsey
Tommy Carlyn & Orchestra
Tommy Payne
Tommy Roe
Vaughn Monroe
Walt Harper
Westinghouse Band
Wild Cherry
Xavier Cugat & his Orchestra

Selected Bibliography

Interviews and Correspondences

Adams, L. Howard. Email correspondence/interview, March 22, 2020

Alioto, Vito & Mary. Personal Interview, 2017-2020

Andra, John. Personal Interview, September 4, 2019

Balzer, Theresa. Personal Interview, September 17, 2019

Beares III, Charles. Personal, Phone Interviews and Email correspondences, 2019-2021

Beck, Ron. Email correspondence/interview, March 19, 2020

Benson, Tom. Phone Interview and Email correspondences, 2018-2019

Binz, Tom. Personal Interview. March 10, 2021

Costello, Mike. Phone Interviews and Email correspondences, 2018-2021

Harton IV, Dr. George. Phone Interviews and Email correspondences, 2017-2021

Henninger, Bill. Email correspondences, November 13, 2017 & February 28, 2019.

Henry, JR. Phone Interview, April 2, 2020

Hilton, Kathy Vettel. Phone Interview and Email correspondences, 2018-2021

Kerr, Scott. Phone Interview and Email correspondences, April 3, 2020, 2020

Kyriazi, Gary. Email correspondence, October 17. 2019

Knoebel, Dick. Phone Interview. November 5, 2020

Linkenheimer III, Bill. Email correspondences, January 23-25, 2019

Macdonald, Elaine Bahr. Email Correspondences January 2021

MacDonald, Jean Burns. Phone Interview, March 29, 2020

Marasti Sr, Joe. Email Correspondence, April 16, 2019

McIlvain, Carol. Phone Interviews and Email correspondences, 2020-2021

McTighe, Paul. Email correspondence/interview, May 6, 2019 & March 14, 2020

Miller, Jim. Phone Interview. April 1, 2020

Moser, Normajean. Email correspondence, June 3, 2019

Musso, Fred. Phone Interview. November 5, 2020

Nofsinger, Jack. Phone Interview, November 3, 2018

Park, Lary. Email correspondences, January, 2021

Quinn, Andy. Personal Interviews, January 15, 2015 & June 19, 2018

Seitz, Al. Interview March 22, 2020

Snyder, Albert. Phone Interview and correspondences, May 8, 2020, 2020-2021

Shurgott, Sam. Phone Interviews and Email correspondences, 2017-2019

Vettel, Erwin. Phone Interview, March 1, 2021

Von Twistern, Janet H. Phone Interviews and Email correspondences, 2017-2021

Wahlster, Rich. Interview February 16, 2018

Walter, Mary Ann. Personal Interview November-December 2019

Westerman, Ron. Email correspondence/interview, March 22, 2020

Zern, Paul. Phone Interview, March 31, 2020; Personal Interview March 20, 2021

Books

"The Book of Prominent Pennsylvanians; a Standard Reference." The Book of Prominent *Pennsylvanians; a Standard Reference*, Leader Publ., 1913, pp. 72–72.

"Encyclopedia of Pennsylvania Biography: Illustrated, Volume 6." New York, Lewis Historical Publishing Company, 1916, Page 126

Costello, Michael E. *Conneaut Lake Park*. Arcadia, 2005.

Croushore, Jeffrey S. *Idlewild*. Arcadia, 2004.

Jacques, Charles J. *Goodbye, West View Park, Goodbye: "Pittsburgh's Most Popular Playground"*. Amusement Park Journal, 1985.

Jacques, Charles J. *Kennywood-- Roller Coaster Capital of the World*. Amusement Park Journal, 1982.

Jacques, Charles J., et al. *More Kennywood Memories*. Amusement Park Journal, 1998.

Butko, Brian. *Kennywood: Behind the Screams: Pocket Edition*. Senator John Heinz History Center, 2016.

Butko, Brian. *Luna: Pittsburgh's Original Lost Kennywood*. Pittsburgh, PA: Senator Joh Heinz History Center, 2017.

Gompel, Greg Van. *Excelsior Amusement Park: Playland of the Twin Cities*. The History Press, 2017.

Hahner, David P. *Kennywood*. Arcadia, 2004.

Hayek, J. and Kuck, E. (2002). *Remembering Toledo's amusement parks*. Flint, Mich.: Kendall Printing.

Futrell, Jim. *Waldameer Park*. Arcadia Publishing, 2013.

Sopko, Jennifer. *Idlewild: History and Memories of Pennsylvania's Oldest Amusement Park*. The History Press, 2018.

Shale, Richard, and Charles J. Jacques. *"Idora Park: the Last Ride of Summer"*. Amusement Park Journal, 1999

Francis, David W., and Diane DeMali Francis. *Cedar Point: The Queen of American Watering Places*. Amusement Park Books, 1995.

Bush, Lee O., and Richard F. Hershey. *Conneaut Lake Park: the First 100 Years of Fun: a Century Spanned*. Amusement Park Books, 1992.

Magazines

Stockinger, Herb. "Hale's Tours Goes Off Track and Into Orbit." *Amusement Park Journal*, 1987, pp. 21–22.

Amusement Business, July 14, 1962 "West View Banks on Kiddieland, Ballyhoo"

Amusement Business, September 7, 1963 "West View Closing TWO Days Each Week"

Billboard Magazine 1905-1959

Newspapers

The Daily Morning Post (Pittsburgh, PA)

The Pittsburgh Daily Commercial (Pittsburgh, PA)

Pittsburgh Daily Post (Pittsburgh, PA)

The Pittsburgh Dispatch (Pittsburgh, PA)

News & Observer (Raleigh, NC)

Pittsburgh Post-Gazette (Pittsburgh, PA)

Pittsburgh Daily Post (Pittsburgh, PA)

Pittsburgh Press (Pittsburgh, PA)

Buffalo Courier (Buffalo, NY)

Pullman Herald (Pullman, Washington)

The Evening Republican (Meadville, PA)

Pittsburgh Weekly Gazette (Pittsburgh, PA)

Harrisburgh-Telegraph (Harrisburg, PA)

Pittsburgh Sun-Telegraph (Pittsburgh, PA)

North Hills News Record (Pittsburgh, PA)

Star Gazette (Elmira, NY)

Other Sources

Charles and Betty Jacques Amusement Park Collection, 1873-2016. Collection no. 521, Special Collections Library, Pennsylvania State University, State College, Pennsylvania

Vettel Family Papers and Photographs, c1895-1995, MSS 1086, Thomas and Katherine Detre Library and Archives, Senator John Heinz History Center

Personal Written Memories

Paul Ley West View Park – The Magic Kingdom before there was a Magic Kingdom

Chuck Brunner – My Remembrances of West View Park

John Andra – West View Park & Danceland

Mary Ann Walter – West View Park

Tom Benson – Memories of West View Park

Correspondences & Records

Letters to T.M. Harton, Ligonier Valley Railroad Records, 1895-1896

T.M. Harton Company Correspondences, Board Meeting & Stockholder Meeting Minutes, Business Accounts & Ledgers, and Records 1905-1965

Various West View Park Company Correspondences, Board Meeting & Stockholder Meeting Minutes, and Records 1906-1981

West View Whip Co. Board of Directors Meeting minutes 1928-1952

Brochures and Other Publications

West View Park promotional brochure, 1920s

West View Park promotional brochure, 1950s

West View Park promotional brochure, 1960s

George J. Keller's Wild Animals promotional brochure

Photograph Credits

Chapter 1: Origins of the T.M. Harton Company

1. T.M. Harton portrait young – Harton/Beares Family.
2. First Ferris Wheel – Photo Antiquities Museum of Photographic History, Pittsburgh, PA.
3. George Harton II portrait – Harton/Beares Family.
4. Switchback Railway drawing – Paul and Bridget Zern Collection.
5. PGH Point - Prints and Photographs Division, Library of Congress, Washington, D.C.
6. Allegheny River 'Smoke City PGH' – Prints and Photographs Division, Library of Congress, Washington, D.C.
7. T.M. Harton Company 1912 ad - *Billboard Magazine* / M. Funyak Collection.
8. PGH Point - Prints and Photographs Division, Library of Congress, Washington, D.C.
9. Harton Family Tree – Harton/Beares Family.

Chapter 2: Entrepreneur and Growing Success

1. T.M. Harton Company 1906 Billboard Ad – Billboard Magazine / M. Funyak Collection.
2. Coney Island Dips – Vettel Family Papers and Photographs, Detre Library and Archives Division, Senator John Heinz History Center, Pittsburgh, PA.
3. Walbridge Park postcard - John Caruthers collection, National Amusement Park Historical Association (NAPHA) Archives, Lombard, IL.

4. Walbridge Park Postcard - John Caruthers collection, National Amusement Park Historical Association (NAPHA) Archives, Lombard, IL.

5. Athletic Park Newspaper Advertisement – *Buffalo Evening Times* / M. Funyak Collection.

6. Athletic Park Buffallo NY - John Caruthers collection, National Amusement Park Historical Association (NAPHA) Archives, Lombard, IL.

7. Conneaut Lake Park Carousel B&W Photo – Harton/ Beares Family.

8. Conneaut Lake Park Carousel color photo_1998 – Samuel Shurgott Collection.

9. Conneaut Lake Park Jack Rabbit Coaster – Harton/Beares Family.

10. Waldameer carousel 14 – Charles and Betty Jacques Amusement Park Collection, 00521, Special Collections Library, Pennsylvania State University, State College, PA.

11. Rock Springs Park Postcard – Michael E. Costello.

12. Paxtang Park Postcard - Charles and Betty Jacques Amusement Park Collection, 00521, Special Collections Library, Pennsylvania State University, State College, PA.

13. T.M. Harton Theater Co. Newspaper – *Star-Gazette* (Elmira, NY) / M. Funyak Collection.

14. Atlantic City Coaster – Harton/Beares Family.

15. Fred and Josiah Pearce photo – Pearce Family.

16. Erwin Vettel Portrait – Vettel Family Papers and Photographs, Detre Library and Archives Division, Senator John Heinz History Center, Pittsburgh, PA.

17. Erwin Vettel Portrait - Vettel Family Papers and Photographs, Detre Library and Archives Division, Senator John Heinz History Center, Pittsburgh, PA.

18. Canadian expo Scenic Auto Dips – Vettel Family Papers and Photographs, Detre Library and Archives Division, Senator John Heinz History Center, Pittsburgh, PA.

19. Toronto Scenic Dips Construction – Vettel Family Papers and Photographs, Detre Library and Archives Division, Senator John Heinz History Center, Pittsburgh, PA.

20. Waldameer color carousel postcard – Michael E. Costello.

21. Waldameer color figure eight postcard – Michael E. Costello.

22. Oakford Park color figure eight postcard – Michael E. Costello.

Chapter 3: Industry Leader to Global Footprint

1. Pittsburgher to build coasters in England – Pittsburgh Press / M. Funyak Collection.

2. Stella and Ed Vettel wedding photo – Kathy Vettel Hilton.

3. Coney Island Carousel – Charles and Betty Jacques Amusement Park Collection, 00521, Special Collections Library, Pennsylvania State University, State College, PA.

4. Coaster Car – Vettel Family Papers and Photographs, Detre Library and Archives Division, Senator John Heinz History Center, Pittsburgh, PA.

5. Andrew Vettel far left – Vettel Family Papers and Photographs, Detre Library and Archives Division, Senator John Heinz History Center, Pittsburgh, PA.

6. Building Coaster Car – Vettel Family Papers and Photographs, Detre Library and Archives Division, Senator John Heinz History Center, Pittsburgh, PA.

7. Coaster Construction Team – Vettel Family Papers and Photographs, Detre Library and Archives Division, Senator John Heinz History Center, Pittsburgh, PA.

8. Coaster – Vettel Family Papers and Photographs, Detre Library and Archives Division, Senator John Heinz History Center, Pittsburgh, PA.

9. Coaster – Vettel Family Papers and Photographs, Detre Library and Archives Division, Senator John Heinz History Center, Pittsburgh, PA.

10. Figure 8 Bahn – Vettel Family Papers and Photographs, Detre Library and Archives Division, Senator John Heinz History Center, Pittsburgh, PA.

11. Dip The Dips – Vettel Family Papers and Photographs, Detre Library and Archives Division, Senator John Heinz History Center, Pittsburgh, PA.

12. Glen Island Dips – Kenny Rutherford Collection.

13. Idora Park Jack Rabbit Station – J.W. Green.

14. Idora Park Jack Rabbit Harton Sign – J.W. Green.

15. Revere Beach – Vettel Family Papers and Photographs, Detre Library and Archives Division, Senator John Heinz History Center, Pittsburgh, PA.

16. Revere Beach – Vettel Family Papers and Photographs, Detre Library and Archives Division, Senator John Heinz History Center, Pittsburgh, PA.

17. Coaster Crew on Lift – Vettel Family Papers and Photographs, Detre Library and Archives Division, Senator John Heinz History Center, Pittsburgh, PA.

18. Newspaper Ad Carpenters - *The Register*, Sandusky, Ohio / M. Funyak Collection.

Chapter 4: Establishing a Home Base 'West View Park'

1. New Park For Pittsburg, Billboard Article – *Billboard Magazine* / M. Funyak Collection.

2. George Harton II portrait – Harton/Beares Family.

3. T.M. Harton II portrait – Harton/Beares Family.

4. A.S. McSwigan portrait – Photo Courtesy of Mary McDonough.

5. West View Park concept art – Harton/Beares Family.

6. Office construction Photo – *Pittsburgh Press* / M.Funyak Collection.

7. F.W. Henninger portrait – Photo Courtesy of Bill Henninger.

8. West View Park Company Letterhead – Harton/Beares Family.

9. Mystic Chute Postcard (ferris wheel/dips in background) - Carol McIlvain

10. Lake Placid Postcard - Carol McIlvain.

11. Early 1900s West View Park Midway Postcard – Harton/Beares Family.

12. Newspaper photo Penny Arcade - *Pittsburgh Press* / Paul and Bridget Zern Collection.

13. Newspaper photo Dining Pavilion - *Pittsburgh Press* / Paul and Bridget Zern Collection.

14. First Band Stage – Charles J. Jacques, Jr. Collection, Pittsburgh Photographic Library, Carnegie Library of Pittsburgh Pennsylvania Department.
15. Original Dance Pavilion Postcard - Charles J. Jacques, Jr. Collection, Pittsburgh Photographic Library, Carnegie Library of Pittsburgh Pennsylvania Department.
16. Dips Construction – Charles J. Jacques, Jr. Collection, Pittsburgh Photographic Library, Carnegie Library of Pittsburgh Pennsylvania Department.
17. Dips Turnaround - Paul and Bridget Zern Collection.
18. Newspaper Photo – Original Carousel – Pittsburgh Press / Paul and Bridget Zern Collection.
19. Pony Track & Bridge – Charles J. Jacques, Jr. Collection, Pittsburgh Photographic Library, Carnegie Library of Pittsburgh Pennsylvania Department.
20. West View Park Ball Grounds Postcard – Paul and Bridge Zern Collection.
21. Bridge/Streetcar Entrance Postcard – Carol McIlvain.
22. Amusement Arena West View Park Postcard – Carol McIlvain .
23. Looking back on Dips Lift Posctard – Carol McIlvain.
24. Boat Landing with Dips Postcard - Paul and Bridge Zern Collection.
25. Figure Eight/Hill/Gazebo Postcard – Carol McCilvain.
26. 1912 Pony Track Postcard Talkie Temple Site – Carol McIlvain.
27. Original Park Stage photo – Paul and Bridget Zern Collection.
28. Color Dance Pavilion Postcard – Carol McIlvain.
29. West View Park Mule Postcard B&W – Harton/Beares Family.
30. West View Park midway 'Speed O Plane' – Harton/Beares Family.

Chapter 5: The Beares Era

1. T.M. Harton Dies In East End Home – *Pittsburgh Daily Post* / M. Funyak Collection.
2. Roller Coaster – Charles L. Miklos 1902-1987.
3. Pony Track 1920s – Paul and Bridget Zern Collection.
4. Dips Turnaround & Lake – Charles L. Miklos 1902-1987.
5. Olive Harton Jones portrait – Harton/Beares Family.
6. T.M. Harton Company Incorporation – Harton/Beares Family.
7. Joy Plane at West View Park - Charles L. Miklos 1902-1987.
8. West View Semi-Pro Football Team – Paul McTighe.
9. West View Park Ballfield Postcard – Paul and Bridget Zern Collection.
10. Original West View Park Administration Office – Gary Schmidecke.
11. Charles Beares II Portrait – Harton/Beares Family.
12. Charles Beares II with park pony – Harton Beares Family.
13. Dips station 1929 – Harton/Beares Family.
14. Roller Coaster First Hill - Charles L. Miklos 1902-1987.
15. Racing Whippet – Harton/Beares Family.
16. West View Park Caterpillar 1920s - Charles L. Miklos 1902-1987.

17. Greyhound Rollercoaster – Pittsburgh Press / M. Funyak Collection.
18. Dips New Turnaround – Gary Schmidecke.
19. Willow Grove Park Thunderbolt – Doug Garner Collection.
20. Conneaut Lake Park Scenic Railway Postcard – Michael E. Costello.
21. John P. Hickey – Ellen Gipko.
22. West View Park Kauffmann's Dept Store Employee Picnic – Kaufmann's Department Store Photographs, Detre Library and Archives Division, Senator John Heinz History Center, Pittsburgh, PA.
23. Zephyr Lift Hill – Photo by Chip Landry.
24. Zephyr First Drop – Photo by Richard Munch.
25. Ed Vettel Jr. and Ivan Murray – Kathy Vettel Hilton.
26. Lakeside Amusement Park Cyclone First drop – John Caruthers collection, National Amusement Park Historical Association (NAPHA) Archives.
27. Lakeside Amusement Park Cyclone – John Caruthers collection, National Amusement Park Historical Association (NAPHA) Archives.
28. Charles Beares II signing Junior Commandos contract 1943 – *Pittsburgh Post-Gazette*/ M. Funyak Collection.
29. Charlie Beares III with his Grandparents – Harton/Beares Family.
30. $75,000 Racing Whippet May 1927 – *Pittsburgh Gazette Times* / M. Funyak Collection.
31. Talkie Temple – Paul and Bridget Zern Collection.
32. Park Men Attend Chicago Convention 1936 – *Pittsburgh Press* / M. Funyak Collection.
33. Family Photo – Mary Alioto / M. Funyak Collection.
34. New Administration Building – Harton/Beares Family.
35. Idlewild Carousel circa 1930s - Charles and Betty Jacques Amusement Park Collection, 00521, Special Collections Library, Pennsylvania State University.
36. Midway Gazebo Photo – Harton/Beares Family.
37. 1930s Photo of West View Roller Coasters – Charles and Betty Jacques Amusement Park Collection, 00521, Special Collections Library, Pennsylvania State University.
38. Municipal Tax Ticket – Michael E. Costello.
39. Clown Icon From Park Issued License Plate Topper – Paul and Bridget Zern Collection.
40. Dips and Lake Placid Postcard – Paul and Bridget Zern Collection.
41. Family Day at the Park – Mary Alioto / M. Funyak Collection.
42. Ferris Wheel on Midway – Paul and Bridget Zern Collection.
43. Family Day at West View Park – Theresa Balzer.
44. Family Day at West View Park – Mary Alioto.
45. Cedar Point High Frolic Station – Vettel Family Papers and Photographs, Detre Library and Archives Division, Senator John Heinz History Center, Pittsburgh, PA.
46. Cedar Point High Frolic roller coaster - Vettel Family Papers and Photographs, Detre Library and Archives Division, Senator John Heinz History Center, Pittsburgh, PA.
47. Conneaut Lake Park Blue Streak – Michael E. Costello.
48. Bridge and Flowers Postcard – Paul and Bridget Zern Collection.
49. Bug and Racing Whippet Postcard – M. Funyak Collection

Chapter 6: The **George Harton Years**

1. George Harton III Portrait – Harton/Beares Family.
2. George Harton III, Ed Vettel Jr, Charlie Beares II – Harton/Beares Family.
3. Carousel Horses – Harton/Beares Family.
4. Ed Sr. and Ed Jr. with Coaster Models – Kathy Vettel Hilton.
5. Ed Sr. and Ed Jr. at dinner– Kathy Vettel Hilton.
6. Racing Whippet – Larry Ward, West View Park photographs and negatives, 1960-1961, Detre Library and Archives Division, Senator John Heinz History Center, Pittsburgh, PA.
7. 1950s West View Park Entrance – Harton/Beares Family.
8. Fledging Flyer next to Dips – Larry Ward, West View Park photographs and negatives, 1960-1961, Detre Library and Archives Division, Senator John Heinz History Center, Pittsburgh, PA.
9. Family on Tilt-a-Whirl – Charles and Betty Jacques Amusement Park Collection, 00521, Special Collections Library, Pennsylvania State University, State College, PA.
10. Picnic Pavilion - Larry Ward, West View Park photographs and negatives, 1960-1961, Detre Library and Archives Division, Senator John Heinz History Center, Pittsburgh, PA.
11. Family Day 1960s – Mary Alioto.
12. Picnic Groves – Larry Ward, West View Park photographs and negatives, 1960-1961, Detre Library and Archives Division, Senator John Heinz History Center, Pittsburgh, PA.
13. Band Leader at Danceland - Jack Nofsinger Collection / Tom Binz.
14. New Danceland – Jack Nofsinger Collection / Tom Binz.
15. Danceland Stage with Band - Courtesy of Brian Cunningham via his Grandfather Edwin Marciniak.
16. Inside Danceland – Harton/Beares Family.
17. Event inside Danceland – Harton/Beares Family.
18. Band posing for Photo on Danceland Stage – Courtesy of Brian Cunningham via his Grandfather Edwin Marciniak.
19. 1948 West View Park School Tickets.
20. 1947 Junior Miss Western PA Pageant at WVP – Harton/Beares Family.
21. Dips, 1080 WPGH, Parking Lot Entrance – Harton/Beares Family.
22. Kathy with Duke – Kathy Vettel Hilton.
23. Talkie Temple Wrestling Match – Harton/Beares Family.
24. Billy Outten - Courtesy of Brian Cunningham via his Grandfather Edwin Marciniak
25. Professor George Keller - Courtesy of Brian Cunningham via his Grandfather Edwin Marciniak.
26. Danceland Performer - Courtesy of Brian Cunningham via his Grandfather Edwin Marciniak.

27. Couple shaking performers hand at Danceland - Courtesy of Brian Cunningham via his Grandfather Edwin Marciniak.
28. Date Night – Mary Alioto.
29. Louis Prima and Frank Yankovic advertisement – M. Funyak Collection.
30. Cuddle Up and Ride-N-Laff circa 1952– Harton Beares Family.
31. Parade at Night – Harton/Beares Family.
32. Walbridge Park Postcard – John Caruthers collection, National Amusement Park Historical Association (NAPHA) Archives.
33. Pirates at West View Park – Larry Ward, West View Park photographs and negatives, 1960-1961, Detre Library and Archives Division, Senator John Heinz History Center, Pittsburgh, PA.
34. George III and Boru with young guest – Harton/Beares Family.
35. The Bavarian Room – Jack Nofsinger Collection / Tom Binz.
36. George IV and Janet on Racing Whippet – Harton/Beares Family.
37. West View Park Employees – Charles and Betty Jacques Amusement Park Collection, 00521, Special Collections Library, Pennsylvania State University, State College, PA.
38. Frank Martin – Elaine (Bahr) Macdonald.
39. Riding a Pony at West View Park – Theresa Balzer.
40. Postcard view of Games Mall – Kathy Vettel Hilton.
41. Dick Newman, George Harton III, John Hickey Sr – Harton/Beares Family
42. George Bodnar – Charles J. Jacques, Jr. Collection, Pittsburgh Photographic Library, Carnegie Library of Pittsburgh Pennsylvania Department.
43. West View Park advertisements – Jack Nofsinger Collection / Tom Binz.
44. Wild Mouse from Dips – Larry Ward, West View Park photographs and negatives, 1960-1961, Detre Library and Archives Division, Senator John Heinz History Center, Pittsburgh, PA.
45. Wild Mouse Sign – Larry Ward, West View Park photographs and negatives, 1960-1961, Detre Library and Archives Division, Senator John Heinz History Center, Pittsburgh, PA.
46. Wild Mouse ride – Larry Ward, West View Park photographs and negatives, 1960-1961, Detre Library and Archives Division, Senator John Heinz History Center, Pittsburgh, PA.
47. Kiddieland re-dedication – Photo Courtesy of Tom Benson.
48. Kiddieland – Charles J. Jacques, Jr. Collection, Pittsburgh Photographic Library, Carnegie Library of Pittsburgh Pennsylvania Department.
49. Antique Cars – Bill Kozup.
50. Boats sign being painted – Jack Nofsinger Collection / Tom Binz.
51. Bill Cardille, Janet at Talkie Temple with Bike winner – Harton/Beares Family.
52. Bill Haley Ad and Rolling Stones Ad – M. Funyak Collection.
53. Beach Boys Danceland advertisement – M. Funyak Collection.
54. Harton Family Photo at Free Act Space – Harton/Beares Family.

55. Riders on Caterpillar – Larry Ward, West View Park photographs and negatives, 1960-1961, Detre Library and Archives Division, Senator John Heinz History Center, Pittsburgh, PA.

56. Ladies in arcade redemption counter - Jack Nofsinger Collection / Tom Binz

57. Kids on Ballfield – Charles and Betty Jacques Amusement Park Collection, 00521, Special Collections Library, Pennsylvania State University, State College, PA.

58. Bike kiddie ride – Larry Ward, West View Park photographs and negatives, 1960-1961, Detre Library and Archives Division, Senator John Heinz History Center, Pittsburgh, PA.

59. Helicopters – Bill Kozup.

60. Huba Huba the Clown – Harton/Beares Family.

61. Midway with Helicopter ride – Larry Ward, West View Park photographs and negatives, 1960-1961, Detre Library and Archives Division, Senator John Heinz History Center, Pittsburgh, PA

62. Ed Jr on Dips Lift Hill - Kathy Vettel Hilton.

63. Bob Vettel inspecting the Helicopter ride – Kathy Vettel Hilton.

64. Inside Committee Room – Courtesy of Brian Cunningham via his Grandfather Edwin Marciniak.

65. Four Freshman at Danceland 1961 – Larry Ward, West View Park photographs and negatives, 1960-1961, Detre Library and Archives Division, Senator John Heinz History Center, Pittsburgh, PA.

66. Boru Hot Dog Promotion – Harton/Beares Family.

67. Pony Track – Larry Ward, West View Park photographs and negatives, 1960-1961, Detre Library and Archives Division, Senator John Heinz History Center, Pittsburgh, PA.

68. Pony Track Employees – Elaine (Bahr) Macdonald.

69. Street Car at WVP next to Danceland - Charles and Betty Jacques Amusement Park Collection, 00521, Special Collections Library, Pennsylvania State University.

70. Free Act Stage – Courtesy of Brian Cunningham via his Grandfather Edwin Marciniak.

71. Carousel Horse - Charles J. Jacques, Jr. Collection, Pittsburgh Photographic Library, Carnegie Library of Pittsburgh Pennsylvania Department.

72. Soda Bar - Jack Nofsinger Collection / Tom Binz.

73. Pony Cart ride - Jack Nofsinger Collection / Tom Binz.

74. Scooter Building circa 1956 – Harton/Beares Family.

75. Girls on Ferris Wheel – Larry Ward, West View Park photographs and negatives, 1960-1961, Detre Library and Archives Division, Senator John Heinz History Center, Pittsburgh, PA.

76. Looper, Bat Chute, Rock O Plane, Tilt-a-Whirl, and Bug – Larry Ward, West View Park photographs and negatives, 1960-1961, Detre Library and Archives Division, Senator John Heinz History Center, Pittsburgh, PA.

77. Ferris Wheel Operator – Larry Ward, West View Park photographs and negatives, 1960-1961, Detre Library and Archives Division, Senator John Heinz History Center, Pittsburgh, PA.

78. Mirror Maze – Larry Ward, West View Park photographs and negatives, 1960-1961, Detre Library and Archives Division, Senator John Heinz History Center, Pittsburgh, PA.

79. Rock-O-Plane - Jack Nofsigner Collection / Tom Binz.

80. Popcorn Box – Jack Nofsinger Collection / Tom Binz.

81. WVP memorabilia – Jack Nofsinger Collection / Tom Binz.

82. Girl receiving cotton candy – Jack Nofsinger Collection / Tom Binz.

83. Flying Scooter – Jack Nofsinger Collection / Tom Binz.

84. Kiddie Whip – Jack Nofsinger Collection / Tom Binz.

85. Up-C Daze – Charles and Betty Jacques Amusement Park Collection, 00521, Special Collections Library, Pennsylvania State University.

86. Dips Turnaround – Jack Nofsinger Collection / Tom Binz.

87. Davey Jones Locker - Charles and Betty Jacques Amusement Park Collection, 00521, Special Collections Library, Pennsylvania State University, State College, PA.

88. Krazy Daisy - Charles and Betty Jacques Amusement Park Collection, 00521, Special Collections Library, Pennsylvania State University, State College, PA.

89. Rides at Night – Charles J. Jacques, Jr. Collection, Pittsburgh Photographic Library, Carnegie Library of Pittsburgh Pennsylvania Department.

90. The Bug at Night – Jack Nofsinger Collection / Tom Binz.

91. Mirror Maze at Night – Jack Nofsinger Collection / Tom Binz.

92. Haunted Swing at Night – Jack Nofsinger Collection / Tom Binz.

93. Park Aerial Photo 1 – Harton/Beares Family.

94. Park Aerial Photo 2 – Harton/Beares Family.

Chapter 7: Jack at the Helm

1. Jack Hickey & Jim Kuhns – Photo Courtesy of Tom Benson.

2. Skip Morrow at Danceland – Photo Courtesy of Tom Benson.

3. Tom Benson & Co-worker – Photo Courtesy of Tom Benson.

4. Chief Jim Miller – Photo Courtesy of Tom Benson .

5. Hat Stand – Photo Courtesy of Tom Benson.

6. Petes Pipers at Danceland – Photo Courtesy of Tom Benson.

7. The Amusement Park movie production – Photo Courtesy of Tom Benson.

8. Danceland fire – Photo Courtesy of Ronald T. Westerman.

9. Danceland fire – Photo Courtesy of Ronald T. Westerman.

10. Danceland flagpole eagle – Kathy Vettel Hilton.

11. Carousel Horse Refurbishment – Jack Nofsinger Collection / Tom Binz.

12. Carousel Horse Refurbishment – Jack Nofsinger Collection / Tom Binz.

13. Skip Morrow & Spin Art – Photo Courtesy of Tom Benson.
14. West View Park Employees – Photo Courtesy of Tom Benson.
15. West View Park Employees – Photo Courtesy of Tom Benson.
16. Ice Ball Stand – Photo Courtesy of Tom Benson.
17. Parking Attendant Scott Kerr – Photo Courtesy of Tom Benson.
18. Jack Hickey - Taken by Joe Olszewski.
19. Employee Credentials – Photo Courtesy of Tom Benson.
20. Racing Whippet – Photo by Frank Czuri.
21. Excited Racing Whippet Riders – Photo by Frank Czuri.
22. West View Park Sign Open Today – Photo Courtesy of Tom Benson.
23. Al Francischiani and Cart Miller – Jean Burns MacDonald.
24. Margaret Habel – Taken by Joe Olszewski.
25. Porky the Paper Eater – Charles and Betty Jacques Amusement Park Collection, 00521, Special Collections Library, Pennsylvania State University, State College, PA.
26. Parking lot Kathy – Photo Courtesy of Tom Benson.
27. Racing Whippet – Photo by Frank Czuri.
28. Racing Whippet – Charles and Betty Jacques Amusement Park Collection, 00521, Special Collections Library, Pennsylvania State University, State College, PA.
29. Racing Whippet first drop – Photo by Frank Czuri.
30. Dips – Photo by Al Snyder.
31. Dips first drop – Photo by Al Snyder.
32. Dips riders – Jean Burns MacDonald.
33. Dips turnaround color – Photo by Frank Czuri.
34. Tempest Operator – Photo by Al Snyder.
35. C.P. Huntington Train – Photo by Al Snyder.
36. West View Park Picnic Raffle – West View Historical Society.
37. Scooter – Jean Burns MacDonald.
38. Park Midway 1970s – Photo by Al Snyder.
39. Trabant at Night – Photo Courtesy of Tom Benson.
40. Talkie Temple with rock band – Photo by Al Snyder.
41. Skip Morrow – Photo Courtesy of Tom Benson.
42. Fountain on Lake – Photo by Al Snyder.
43. Alpine Sky Ride – Al Snyder .
44. West View Park – Al Synder.
45. West View Park Employees – Photo by Al Snyder.
46. Boot Hill – Photo by Al Snyder.
47. Bug – West View Historical Society.
48. Haunted House – Harton/Beares Family.
49. Busy Midway B&W – Charles and Betty Jacques Amusement Park Collection, 00521, Special Collections Library, Pennsylvania State University, State College, PA.

Chapter 8: The Final Season

1. Racing Whippet Bridge– West View Historical Society.
2. Family Photo – Theresa Balzer.
3. Andy Vettel at Kennywood - Vettel Family Papers and Photographs, Detre Library and Archives Division, Senator John Heinz History Center, Pittsburgh, PA.
4. Bob "Bud" Vettel – Kathy Vettel Hilton.
5. Round Up – Charles J. Jacques, Jr. Collection, Pittsburgh Photographic Library, Carnegie Library of Pittsburgh Pennsylvania Department.
6. West View Park Tickets/Final Season – Harton/Beares Family.
7. Haunted House - Charles and Betty Jacques Amusement Park Collection, 00521, Special Collections Library, Pennsylvania State University.
8. Family Photo – Theresa Balzer.
9. Racing Whippet during Fall - John Caruthers collection, National Amusement Park Historical Association (NAPHA) Archives.
10. Dips Brake Run – Charles and Betty Jacques Amusement Park Collection, 00521, Special Collections Library, Pennsylvania State University.
11. Midway Fountain - Jean Burns MacDonald.
12. Carousel Goat – Charles J. Jacques, Jr. Collection, Pittsburgh Photographic Library, Carnegie Library of Pittsburgh Pennsylvania Department.
13. Bob "Bud" Vettel near Dips/Fascination – Kathy Vettel Hilton.
14. West View Park Shopping Center – M. Funyak Collection
15. West View Park Drive street sign – M. Funyak Collection
16. Lion and sign from Waldbridge Park Carousel – Merry Go Round Museum.
17. Panel from WVP first Carousel – M. Funyak Collection
18. Games Mall Neon – Charles and Betty Jacques Amusement Park Collection, 00521, Special Collections Library, Pennsylvania State University, State College, PA.
19. 1970s West View Park Midway – Paul and Bridget Zern Collection
20. West View Park Sticker – Harton/Beares Fmaily.
21. WVP Office Furniture – Carol McIlvain.
22. WVP Employee Reunion - Photo Courtesy of Tom Benson.
23. Racing Whippet – Charles and Betty Jacques Amusement Park Collection, 00521, Special Collections Library, Pennsylvania State University, State College, PA.
24. Kiddieland Entrance - Harton/Beares Family.
25. Jolly Caterpillar – West View Historical Society.
26. Kennywood Jack Rabbit Train – M. Funyak Collection.
27. Kennywood Thunderbolt – M. Funyak Collection.
28. Dips cresting Hill – Charles and Betty Jacques Amusement Park Collection, 00521, Special Collections Library, Pennsylvania State University, State College, PA.
29. Center Slice Pizza – Michael E. Costello.

About the Author

MIKE FUNYAK has worked in the amusement industry for 10 years. His introduction to the industry came when he began working as a Ride Operator at West Mifflin, PA's famous Kennywood Park, while earning a degree from Robert Morris University. It was during his second season there that his passion for amusement parks grew as he spent his down time learning about the park and the industry from Kennywood's Andy Quinn.

Following graduation, Funyak continued his amusement park career path, working for Morey's Piers & Beachfront Water Parks in New Jersey, Fun Fore All Family Fun Park, Cranberry Township, PA, Idlewild & Soak Zone in Ligonier, and DelGrosso's Park/Laguna Splash, Tipton, PA.

Like many in Western Pennsylvania, the author owes part of his very existence to West View Park's Danceland, where his grandparents first met and fell in love.

The author makes his home in the Altoona area where he is Assistant Director of Operations for DelGrosso's Park.

www.ingramcontent.com/pod-product-compliance
Lightning Source LLC
Chambersburg PA
CBHW081654120626
46550CB00010B/2894